1

CREATION & EVOLUTION

plus

NATURAL & POSITIVE LAW

by
Jean-Nil Chabot

CONTENTS

Introduction

INRODUCTION

Experimental science stops at the door of metaphysics and metaphysics at the door of faith. It seems that within the realm of reason alone, there exists between metaphysics and experimental science a gap that the philosophy of nature has not yet been able to fill. It is true that Thomas Aquinas and Aristotle - the great masters of hylomorphism, which provide the embryo of an answer to the problem - saw reality as being at once physical and metaphysical, while taking care to distinguish between the two perspectives. In fact, physics examines the corporal elements in their different forms according to their natures in genesis, while metaphysics focuses on their fixed natures or their essences thereof; from the point of view of Being and of its participant beings. However, since these two sciences have not developed in conjunction with each other they have offered no explanation regarding the passage from Being to beings, from the One to the multiple, from Eternity to time and from time to Eternity. The bridging of these gnostic gaps can hardly be completed without the help of divine revelation. What follows is an attempt to offer a resolution to this problem.

Such a resolution, however imperfect it might be, could be beneficial even for the practical domains where the common good is concerned. One actual concern is the domain of law where an immutable foundation needs to be established. It would help to determine what relationship exists between positive law and natural law and, as well, their foundation in eternal law where faith in divine revelation is concerned.

To explore the problem adequately, one must first recognize that these two sciences (physics, which is an empirical science that uses the process of hypothesis and experimentation; metaphysics *or meta ta phusika: "after physics"*, which uses a process of abstraction and analogy) have a common principle in the sensible universe. Both sciences must rely on the tangible reality of Creation to succeed in perceiving Being-in-itself as the source of universal knowledge. While maintaining their distinction, both are needed to unveil the process of Creation in its unique reality in spite of the transcendence imposed on the finite by the incommensurable Infinite. Analogy is not enough, by itself, to recompose in the intellect the bridge between Being and beings, because it lacks the logical sequence needed to link the Creator to the reality of material and spiritual substances. On the other hand, because finite beings are participants of the Infinite Being, the latter is immanent to them and this aspect appears as an opening to the liaison we seek. Thus a light seems available to illuminate the mysterious way by which ideas become reality.

PART I

Nothing out of nothing

Since physics and metaphysics have in common the existence of reality as an object of knowledge, can one not assume that they complement one another in the search for a comprehensive understanding of the universe in relation to its being and becoming? The purpose of this essay is to propose a way of understanding the deployment of all existence from the First Cause by means of these two disciplines, thus allowing to glimpse the link between them. Edith Stein said the same thing about various philosophical disciplines :

> Basically, all issues can be brought back to ontological problems and all philosophical disciplines become part of a large ontology or metaphysics. Because each being should be what it is, its mode of being, essence and existence, extent and type of its knowledge and of its appetites, the truth that is accessible to it and the perfection to which it can attain belongs to God. And so logic, critique, ethics are included, according to their material content, in the ontology even though, in another form, taken normatively, we can can consider them as autonomous disciplines.[1]

From a similar perspective, Fernand Van Steenberghen gives a prominent place to metaphysical knowledge by recognizing the Infinite Being as creative cause of the beings that form the universe :

> Metaphysics ends with the affirmation of the infinite Being, the creative cause, personal and providential of the universe; the problem of God is both the hidden spring and the crowning of

---

[1]Stein, Edith, *Phénoménologie et philosophie chrétienne*, (Phenomenology and Christian philosophy), (Trans. J.-N. C.) , Les Editions du Cerf , Paris , 1987, p . 42.

this research. This affirms the prominent place which comes to metaphysical knowledge in an integral humanism ...[2]

From any demonstration which is in the order of nature, a question arises: Does God exist or does He not exist? For, if He exists, everything comes from him, and if He does not exist, nature is its own god and its own creator, which is to say that the universe originated by chance. Augustin Bernard, among others, was offended by the suggestion that chance could be a substitute for the idea of Creation:

> "Are they mocking us?", he writes, "to eliminate the God-hypothesis (since this is the unspoken intent of the question) they build this fantastic novel of a "frozen" or living tiny microscopic algae formed by chance in the bottom of a swamp or in the oceanic environment, and that, still by chance, the same creature having resisting all causes of destruction, became, always by chance, more complex in the vast tree of plant and animal species in which the stubborn permanence of the Type continually resists the deciduousness of individuals... "[3]

Since we must place the existence of God in a philosophical heritage and the *perennial philosophy* that prevails in the research undertaken here does not allow for any proof of the non-existence of God, because it would then remove from the discourse the concept of cause, which is a principle of the same philosophical development, only the arguments in favour of God's existence will compel the mind. Those arguments are not lacking and Thomas Aquinas offers five of them in his *Summa Theologica*. Among them, I quote the one which is based on the doctrine of causality:

---

[2]Fernand Von Steenberghen, *Ontology*, Beatrice-Nauwelaerts Editions, Paris, 1966, p.6

[3]Bernard, Augustin, *Noos,* Éditions du Scorpion, Paris, 1958, p.139

"There is no cause without effect. We can observe in the world around us that nothing is the cause of its own causality but each one of them depends on another. If a thing could be its own cause it would mean that it could precede itself, which is absurd. In addition, the sequence of causes that ensues one from another must end because in this series of causes a previous thing causes another which is an intermediary and that intermediary (whether composed of one thing or more) causes a final effect. Since by eliminating a cause one eliminates its effects, it is impossible to have a final effect or an intermediate cause without a first cause. If there is no stop of the series, nor a first cause, there will not be, either, an intermediate cause. This is contrary to what we observe in the world. We must therefore assume that there is a first cause which we call God."[4]

Jacques Maritain suggests a sixth argument for the existence of God, which he calls existential. This is not a new proof, but "the eternal path of human reason to approach God." He explains, as follows, this " reasoning without words, whose vital concentration and speed we risk to betray by expressing it in an articulated manner":

"First, I see that my being is subject to death and secondly that it depends on the whole of nature, that is, the universal whole of which I am a part. The Being-with-nothingness, which is my own being, implies, in order to be, a Being-without-nothingness, that is, an absolute existence, which I confusedly perceive wrapped in my primordial intuition of existence. The universal whole is also being-with-nothingness by the fact that I am a part of it, so that, since it does not exist by itself, there is another Whole, - separate - another Being, transcendent and self-sufficient and even unknown in Itself, who activates all beings, who is Being-without-nothingness, that is to say by Being in itself."[5]

---

[4] See *Summa Theologica*, I, q. 2 a. 3.

This phenomenological argument Edith Stein has, herself, restated in her own way, according to what Florent Gaboriau wrote in his book, Edith Stein philosophe:

> "In accordance with a widespread tradition, the starting point used by Edith Stein would have the benefit of offering a convenient shortcut, simple as it is, towards the Essential. We are assured, under the pretext that our being includes some 'non-being', that we are to discover in it 'the idea of a pure Being', which excludes 'no longer' of a past as well as the 'not yet' of the future, and which is thus conceived as Eternal."[6]

In other words, in order to be, things that are in a state of potentiality require the actuality of an unchanging Being.

Ens and verum convertuntur. Consequently, we must admit that the material substances that we know cannot exist without a Creator since in all real beings that we know there is a difference between essence and existence and their union cannot be explained without admitting a cause whose essence and existence are identical. This is Sertillanges' argument which asserts that "all beings except God (have) to be created, because they do not have in themselves the reason of their place in existence (and) this is what is meant by the famous distinction between essence and existence." And the philosopher explains that "it is not a question of setting apart an essence having no existence or a real being having no essence (...) , but of emphasizing a heteronomy between the fact of being what we are and the fact of being actually posited in existence." "In this regard," he adds, "the existence occurs to the essence (accidit) and

---

[5]Maritain, Jacques, *Raison and Raisons*, Egloff, Paris, 1948, p. 172. (Trans. J.-N. C.)
[6]Ref. Sertillanges, A. D.. *L'idée de création et ses retentissements en philosophie*, Aubier, Paris , 1945, p. 44. (Trans. J.-N. C.).

God produces the occurrence." "Such is the object", he concludes, "of the creative act".[7]

The same author adds that "Christian tradition has always understood Creation as a participation in God from the double point of view of *intelligibility*[8] and of *being*, in other words, in *essence* and in *existence*, with this difference that the *essence*, by itself, did not need to be created since, as such, it is only one of the ways in which the fully divine can be participated and it is joined as one reality with the divine essence itself." And "it is because this participated essence did not have its own right to exist that it had to be brought to existence by creation".[9] Thus, the essences exist in God and are not created. If they depended on the pure will of the Creator, as Descartes had believed, they would be without intrinsic necessity and the uncertainty of their determination and of their permanence that would result, would no longer provide the basis for science.

Assuming the existence of God and of Creation one must recognize, as a consequence, that the world is not the product of chance, but that it comes from the essences or ideas that are in God. If it were a matter of chance, one could not get the *idea*[10] of the result before the

---

[7]Idea in Latin is *forma*. Since, in modern language, the word *form* is added to that of *idea* a nuance needs to be introduced between the two words. As Thomas Aquinas often exemplifies, we can think of the architect as an example to denote this nuance. If we say that the architect has the *idea* of a building we see it represented in a general way. But if we say that the architect has in mind the form of that building, this denotes something more specific and is closer to the conception of a plan.Intelligibility and essence can be, in this case, referred to as *idea*. As for "being", in the context of something brought into *physical reality*, it can be referred to *energy*.

[8]Sertillanges, A.D., *L'idée de création...*, p. 86

[9]The Efficient Cause must be the actuality of what it actualizes, as fire is the actuality of the heat that it actualizes in an object. Thus, Creation is virtually in God before its actualization, just as the heat from the object is in the fire before its actualization in the object.

production was completed while the agent, on the other hand, produces things according to the ideas he already has. From the material substances that we know, we deduce that limited essences, such as energy[11] and form, are distinctions or determinations introduced in God's infinite Essence; in fact, they are only modes of His existence.

Thomas Aquinas affirms that "it is by no means necessary that all that intelligence distinguishes be as distinct in reality: intelligence apprehends things not according to their own mode, but according to its own mode, so that material things, which are inferior to our intellect, are in our intelligence, in a simpler manner than they are in themselves. On the contrary, the angelic substances being superior to our intelligence, the latter cannot apprehend them according to what they are in themselves, but in its own way, that is to say, in the way in which it grasp compound things."[12] In this way we can say that spirit and energy are *of* God, but *in* Him they exist indistinctly, engulfed in divine unity. The application of form gives them a distinct existence in relation to the other created beings as well as in relation to God.

Since pure energy is not yet matter, it cannot be limited by quantity, yet it has a limited essence such as that of pure spirits or the human soul. It functions in a way similar to that of soul in its union with with matter (or life with matter). In the vegetative and animal life, the soul is

---

[10]Idea in Latin is *forma*. Since, in modern language, the word *form* is added to that of *idea* a nuance needs to be introduced between the two words. As Thomas Aquinas often exemplifies, we can think of the architect as an example to denote this nuance. If we say that the architect has the *idea* of a building we see it represented in a general way. But if we say that the architect has in mind the form of that building, this denotes something more specific and is closer to the conception of a plan.

[11]Energy is the source of velocity and time and even identifies with them.

[12]Thomas d'Aquin, *Summa Theologica*: I, q. 12, a. 5

so (intimately) united to matter that the disintegration of one causes the death of both. This happens also to man's animal soul, but not to his spiritual soul. Nevertheless, the natural life of man puts quantitative limits to his spiritual parts creating individual persons as a result. When man dies, his material animal life disappears, but the life of his spiritual soul remains along with the characteristics acquired by its union with matter. Later on, at the resurrection, the whole of human life will be restored, but then the spirit will assume what used to be material and a whole and complete man will arise, but in an immaterial, immortal state.

The angel is the living form of a mind formed according to a species. In the *animal man* there is the soul, the living form of a matter formed according to a species individuated by its accidents, a spiritual form, itself formed by the life of the soul which receives it. This, however, does not apply to accidental multiplication by material propensity, which does not happen substantially and does not result from the marriage of substantial forms such as light and energy or matter and life. Rather accidental multiplication is the result of accidental forms qualifying the substantial forms, such as the different colours of light or the different races of the human genus. Rather, the human soul substantially united to matter, possesses a corruptible form of life, but, moreover, as in the angel, the mind, formed as spirit and united to the soul is invited to participate in the divine life.

When we say that God "creates from nothing", is it to mean that the things he creates are not already within Himself in a certain way, but rather that He draws them from "non-being"? Would it be rather to mean that *He creates from nothing that would already be in existence outside of Himself*? God is the totality of Being and nothing that exist or is possible can be outside of Him, not even the idea of nothing, because all beings, including ideas, are participants of Being and cannot "be" from nothing. Thomas Aquinas admits to that when he says : "Matter and form *pre-exist in God virtually*, as in the primordial cause of both."[13]

It is important to notice that Aquinas uses the expression "pre-exist...virtually". Elsewhere (q. 40, a1), he wrote: "We must consider not only the emanation of a particular being from a particular agent, but also the emanation of all being from the universal cause, which is God; and this emanation we designate by the name of creation." And again (ibid a. 3.): "Although there is no universal nor particular in God, *nor form and matter,* in reality, nevertheless, as regards the mode of signification there is a certain likeness of these things in God.

As for the *nothing-in-itself,* it cannot exist, nor can it be known by itself - it is only known by its opposite: that which exist. And even if "nothing" could be conceived as existing as "non-being," it would not be possible to create being from it without going, along the creating process, through a mixture of being and "non-being", which is absurd, unless it is understood as Maritain understands it. His idea of "Being with non-being", does not mean drawn out of nothing, which necessitates a mixture, but rather it means that it was created with a deprivation of being or as becoming. However, it would have been necessary that some being already existed; some potential material being, or being in deprivation of many forms, according to the concept developed by Aristotle to provide an answer to the ontological inertia of Parmenides.

Bergson would have seen the impossibility of creation from nothing in the same light, since he wrote, in Creative Evolution, that "the idea of nothing, if we claim to see in it the abolishment of all things, is an idea that is destructive of itself and is reduced to a single word."[14] Such an

---

[13]Summa Theologica , I, q. 117, a. 3.
[14]Bergson, Henri, *L'Évolution Créatrice*, Presses Universitaires de France, Paris, 1907, p. 297. Trans. J.-N. C.

idea of the abolishment of all things may probably manifest the same character as that of a square circle"[15]. Moreover, in the case of the idea of an object conceived as "not existing" "there is more in that idea than in the idea of the same object conceived as "existing" because the idea of the object that "does not exist" is necessarily the idea of the "existing" object with, in addition, the representation of an exclusion of this object by the actual reality taken as a whole"[16].

Thomas Aquinas explains "creation from nothing" differently; he writes:

> We must consider not only the emanation of a particular being from a particular agent, but also the emanation of all being from the universal cause, which is God; and this emanation we designate by the name of creation. Now what proceeds by particular emanation, is not presupposed to that emanation; as when a man is generated, he was not before, but man is made from "not-man," and white from "not-white." Hence if the emanation of the whole universal being from the first principle be considered, it is impossible that any being should be presupposed before this emanation. For nothing is the same as no being. Therefore as the generation of a man is from the "not-being" which is "not-man," so, creation, which is the emanation of all being, is from the "not-being" which is "nothing[17]." That is, nothing outside of the first Cause.

Considering what precedes, it appears to suit reason better to conclude that the world was created by and from an Infinite Spiritual Being than to seek a logical argument for the demonstration of its becoming from nothing. No thing comes from no-thing. Neither can the Creative Spiritual Being create anything from no-thing, which is a

---

[15]Ibid. 280
[16]Ibid. , P. 286
[17]*Summa Th.* Part I, Q 44 a 2

contradiction in terms, for "creating from..." requires an indirect object, that is, a thing. God must create from Himself. Creation was always in the mind of the Creative Spirit,[18] whom we call God, and this Infinite Spirit must have always existed. If the universe were not created, it should have always existed, but we observe that this is not possible - unless by an eternal return - because the matter composing it is always in motion, that is to say something in potentiality of something else and, as we have seen, potentiality requires an agent in order to become actual. And, matter could not exist in an eternal return without a First Cause, which does not have a potentiality to be in another form. Because matter is composed of potentiality and act, it cannot be eternal, since this composition is the principle of time and the opposite of eternity. Pure actuality alone can be eternal. In ideas, there is no composition because they are separated from matter. However, we can assign eternity to them only in dependence of the Oneness of God, for eternity does not belong to the multiple. The term Eternity expresses the general and the exclusive, so that there can be only one Eternity. "All is one and all is diverse" said Heraclitus, but in terms of relationship, it is the diversity that proceeds from the One and not the reverse, so the diverse multiplicity cannot constitute the one eternity.

Considered in relation to the realization of subsequent substances through the addition of forms, energy in its first form has been called *prime matter,* which is particularly appropriate for the physical point of view, or *full potency,* which may be more appropriate for an abstract point of view. However, from both points of view, in order that this full potency or first formed energy (mother of all other material substances) be realized, as was just seen, an agent is needed, who is Pure Actuality, One who is Being-in-itself. Matter, like any other creatures such as *separate substances* (i.e. angels) always depends

---

[18]God is not in time, for the Infinite can not be contained, but time is virtually in God because nothing exists outside of the Infinite.

on the Creator Agent. And since the latter exists *ab aeterno* his creatures could be created *ab aeterno,* according to Emile Filion. In the following text, this philosopher argues that this implies no contradiction :

> Let no one say that Creation *ab aeterno* implies a contradiction, because this contradiction could only come from these two hypothesis: either the notion of Creation required that the Creator existed before there was a creature; or that nothing was before the creation except the Creator. But, the concept of Creation requires neither one or the other of these two things; even if the Creator and the creature had coincided eternity in existence, it would nonetheless be true that the creature, by a necessity of nature inscribed in the depths of his entity, would have always been dependent on the Creator; on the other hand, when we say that Creation was made out of *nothing*, it does not mean that before Creation there was a period during in which there existed only the Creator; but in this expression the preposition *of* simply means that the whole entity of the creature was produced by Creation, without any pre-existing subject that would have been the matter from which came the creature; this concept of creation remains whole, even in the case of the Creation *ab aeterno.*[19]

Thomas Aquinas himself admits that matter "as the subject of generation and corruption is incorruptible"[20] although it is "not infinite absolutely speaking" as he explained in the following paragraph:

> Prime matter does not exist by itself in nature, since it is not actually being, but potentially only; hence it is something con-created rather than created. Nevertheless, prime matter even as

---

[19]Filion, Émile, *Éléments de philosophie thomiste*, Congrégation of Notre-Dame, Montreal, 1950, Volume II, p.144 . Trans. J.-N. C.
[20]Summa Theologica, 1, q. 104 a.4.

a potentiality is not *absolutely* infinite, but relatively, because its potentiality extends only to natural forms.[21]

If pure energy has no form to limit it, in what way is it limited and not Infinite? We can only hypothesize that it is limited in a way similar to that of the pure spirit (angels, separate substances) It may be so because of limited non-material qualities and this we can only know by abstraction. However, abstraction does not mean non-existence. The unlimited energy becomes limited when form is applied to it. The result is matter or prime matter.

One can postulate, with Thomas Aquinas that, as a universal potentiality underlying all its transformations, matter is incorruptible. On the other hand, it is not absolutely contradicting Aquinas to say that abstracted and released from its initial form, it is infinite in the sense of being non-measurable. If secondary material forms were to disappear, matter will be reduced to its universal state – that of pure energy - and it would have become alone of its kind, but it would not be reduce to nothing. Rather, such an eventuality would mean a simple return to universal material potentiality or energy that is not contained. But if the determination of energy were to disappear within the Eternal Essence of God, the essence or idea of energy would also disappear within the Eternal Being. It is not, therefore, energy as essence that is implied when Aquinas speaks of finitude, but its union with form. With that, the question of non-existence of matter without form is resurfacing.

We could say that what does not exist in reality cannot contribute to being. However, we must admit that matter could have had a virtual existence before becoming a reality. When Thomas Aquinas acknowledges that any creature "can act only on a pre-required

---

[21]Ibid., Q7, a.2 Sol.3

subject[22]," he is admitting that any change of form requires energy previously formed as subject. It is true that God does not need a subject outside of himself to do his creative work because He is the Being participated of all material substances and he virtually possesses all subjects within Himself. Thomas Aquinas says it in a certain way when he writes that "if a composite thing be produced, it is likened to God by way of a virtual inclusion."[23] This does not exempt the need for any existence to have Infinite Being as principle. Energy formed into matter is a subject participant of Being according to a particular aspect, which is the active potentiality (or force, or any other name that can be given to the divine attribute it represents). Since the term *prime matter* already implies a composition which includes energy and something else, it cannot be one of the underlying causes of material substances. If the term was appropriate, it would mean that something exists by virtue of its compound and some of its compound, such as saying that water exists by virtue of water and hydrogen. The something that participates in the formation of matter is passive potency because of its appetite for the form, but by its union with the latter it acquires a potency capable of action. Thus, a material substance can be understood as a measure of contained energy.

Hans Meyer exposes the problem in the text as follows:

> Aristotle arrived at the idea of prime matter by a progressive process of abstracting all positive determination from the substratum, and he actualized the resulting idea because of his belief in the parallelism between thought and being. The concept, however, gives rise to metaphysical difficulties. Absolute lack of being and real existence are not reconcilable. A thing cannot be a prerequisite without being something positive.

---

[22]. Ibid ., a. 2 .
[23]. I, q . 105, a. 1

In the realm of reality, the concept of matter is an impossible middle between being and non-being. The argument that matter does not exist without a form is not sufficient to save it. Matter and form are really the product of an illegitimate conclusion by analogy from art to nature; they are the result of an exaggerated belief in the parallelism between thought and being.

It is instructive to note that both Aristotle and St. Thomas were forced to abandon the original concept of matter when they came to explain the actual processes of being in nature. Instead of pure potency we find a concrete matter with certain properties and dispositions which plays an essential part in the actualization of a thing. Some have tried unsuccessfully to save the theory by arguing that the ultimate metaphysical principles do not appear on the surface in the process of becoming.

Other considerations seem to make the theory of matter and form untenable. If matter is filled with a striving for a form, if it acts as the cause of certain qualities and imperfections, and as the principle of *individuation*[24], it cannot be a pure potency and the middle between being and non-being. Furthermore, the substantial form does not have a pure potency as its substratum, because at the death of organisms when the soul-form departs, a corpse remains instead of prime matter. The much derided *form cadaverica* which St. Thomas was forced to invent is a mere subterfuge. As a Christian thinker, he was obliged to accord prime matter some kind of being since it was the product

---

[24]Thomas Aquinas's theory of individuation is often misunderstood. Aquinas does hold that the principle of individuation for material things is matter, but (contrary to what seems to be a common belief) this is not his whole account of individuation. Matter is the principle of individuation in material things insofar as matter is not shareable by many, since it is the first subject not existing in another. Hence Aristotle says that if the Idea were separate "it would be something, that is, an individual, which it would be impossible to predicate of many."

of divine creation and reflected the divine Being even though it was a weak being, a *debile esse.* Plato had not provided an idea for matter, but St. Thomas could not avoid providing some kind of idea in God, since there must be a resemblance in God of each of His creatures. He did not, however, admit a complete idea for matter but only an idea for the composite made up of matter and form. But after all, even a *debile esse* is being and not reconcilable with pure potency.[25]

Finally, as a conclusion to what precedes, we can say that God creates by means of ideas and forms which could be said to be *determinations within His essence.* It is important to note that a *determination* is never without that which is being determined, that is. the idea. For example the builder has the idea of a house. Then, by creating a plan for this house he determines what form the house will take.

For the purpose of clarity, the first determining act of creation, by which a separate entity in its essence emerges from the Infinite Essence, will be referred to as the *determining form.* Separate substances such as angel, energy, soul are different effects of different determining forms. Visible light is the first form of energy and produces visible matter. Energy without light is dark energy. Matter formed by invisible light produces dark matter. The formless and void Earth of the Book of Genesis can be understood as energy not yet united to the form of visible light. The visible matter will accept *individuating forms* that will multiply it.[26]

In his creating act, therefore, God first gives a determination to an idea that is within Himself. When a determination is applied within an

---

[25]Hans Meyer, *The Philosophy of St. Thomas Aquinas*, Trad. ang., B. Herder Book Co., Londre, 1945, p. 70.

[26] It could be said that he gives it an *essence.*

undetermined spiritual idea and united to an intellectual form, a substance is realized as an angel (or *separate substance,* as Aristotle would call it). When, on the other hand, a determination is applied to the idea of energy its form appears and produces a non-quantified energy which Aristotle would call *prime matter* (matter lacking a quantifying form). True matter is realized when God unites it to a quantifying form. Then, He makes his Creation evolve by a gradual multiplication of forms. Man has the forms of matter, soul and of spirit. Soul is life: plant life, (plant soul) and animal (beast) life (animal soul) These are soul-lives that die with their bodies.

From the biblical narrative we read: "In the beginning, when God created the heavens and the earth, the earth (matter) was a formless (pure energy) wasteland (see Aquinas re. *formless matter*), and darkness (dark energy) covered the abyss..." Then God said "Let there be light (form)", and there was light (matter could be seen). God saw that light was good, and God divided light from darkness (God differentiates between pure energy, i.e.: *darkness-* and form- i.e.: *light.*) When matter (form & energy) disintegrates at the prime level of its composition, light (form) and heat (energy) are released. Light is received by the sense of sight and heat by the sense of touch.

"*Evening came and morning came: the first day.*" Augustine wrote that "the heaven recorded as made on the first day is the formless spiritual nature, and that the heaven of the second day is the corporeal heaven."[27] As for the formless and void earth, it will be, following the same logic, the formless material nature.

First God gives determination to energy and form within himself. By the union of these two determinations matter issues from God, and yet remains within the scope of his Being. Yet matter is transcended by God since He is Infinite while matter is finite. The effect of this

---

[27](Gen. ad lit. i.9)

action is a virtual physical universe, which will become reality when *energy* is given its first *form*. But, even before this, according to medieval philosophers, a formless matter issues. But if matter is already energy and form, formless matter would simply be pure energy, that is, energy without form. It would be an energy that has not extension or dimension, therefore not contained nor not quantified. This is supported by the scientific discovery of dark energy, an energy that seems to be the source of an increasingly expanding universe.

The first verse of the Bible give us an indication that the first form, that which gives dimension to energy, would be **light**. Science appears to agree with the biblical account in suggesting that when united to light, energy gains the limiting dimensions that make it material. This union, in turn, limits the light itself by virtue of the energetic limitations. Therefore they quantify one another as factors of matter.

"Meanwhile a mighty wind swept over the waters" (God's spirit producing great movement as form and energy are united to create matter)." God did not leave his creation to fend for itself. From the beginning He produced it according to His plan and made it grow. First it was pure matter, then life - plant life followed by animal life - and finally the intellect. He never stopped watching over his Creation.

PART II

All things out of the One

IDEA
(a determination by Infinite Being within Itself)
↓
essences of determined being
↓ ↓
FORCE & FORM
↓ ↓
ENERGY + LIGHT
↓
MATTER (*reality*)

How does matter appear in the process of creation? First, let us acknowledge that energy and form exist eternally and virtually in God as ideas. When God gives determination to energy and form within himself, the effect of this action is a virtual physical universe, which will become *real* when *energy* is given its first *form*. Before this reality, according to some medieval philosophers, a formless matter issues. However, *formless matter,* if considered from the understanding of *reality* as was illustrated above, would be a contradiction in terms, because matter is already a composite that includes *form,* and a thing cannot have form and not have it at the same time. Therefore, if matter is already energy and form, formless matter would simply be pure energy, that is, energy without form. And since the first form that marries energy is quantity, it would be an energy that has no extension nor dimension, therefore not contained. This is supported by the scientific discovery of dark energy, an energy that seems to be the source of an increasingly expanding universe.

But between the ideas and their substances there are stages of creation. Forms proceed from the divine ideas, that is to say, they are limited essences having received a determination within the Infinite Divine essence. They are separate substances: angel, energy, light...; the angel is spirit, energy is force and light is form. Light (or radiation) is the carrier of energy. Hence when a hydrogen atom is split, it releases light and energy... when a match is stroked and bursts into flame, it release light and energy (heat). Thus, science agrees with the biblical account, which seems to suggest that the first form would be *light.* When united to light, energy gains quantity which limits it as matter. This union, in turn limits light by virtue of the energetic limitations. Therefore they quantify one another as matter.

So, from a scientific point of view, light could be the first form applied to energy because it is dimensional and being so, it allows the measurement of celestial bodies, the distances that separate them, and even their ages. It is also known that *light* travels in waves and its wavelength - the distance from one wave "crest" to the next - determines the colour of the light. If one looks closely, however, one can see that the light spreads out just like other waves do - say a water wave passing through a little passage. This becomes particularly noticeable if one looks at light that has passed through a narrow slit. However, the wavelength of visible light is so small that it can produce beams travelling in straight lines that barely spreads out.

From the phenomenon of reflection it can also be deduced that light has extension. When light bounces off of something it is reflected. This is what one sees when looking at the mirror and also at most things around us. In order to reach one's eyes, light bounces off the object in view and changes its direction. It can also bounce off of particles (like water droplets) in the air, which is why one may be able to see beams of sunlight on a foggy day.

Another property which suggests that light has dimension is refraction. This is what happens when light passes from one medium into another. Then the light will bend or, as it usually does, it will split in two - some of it reflecting off the surface, and some of it going through. The light that goes through bends at the surface. The angle of the bend depends on the composition of the media. For example, the angle will be less when it goes from air into glass than when it goes from air into water.

This picture is of light passing through a piece of glass:

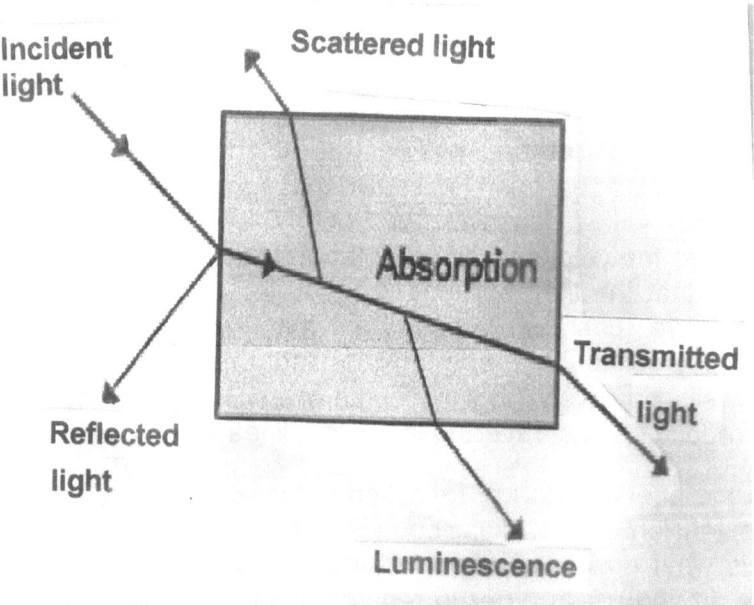

Some of the light can be seen bending and going through the glass (refraction), and some of it can be seen bouncing off of the surface of the glass (reflection). The first verse of the Bible appears to be in conformity with what is explained here, as it affirms that "in the beginning God created the heavens and the earth. The earth was a formless void, and darkness was upon the face of the deep." (Genesis, 1,1) So, the earth, although it was a physical whole, could not be seen not only because it was *formless* for lack of the light that gives it dimension, but would also have been invisible because it did not possess *visible light,* that is, light with the wavelength cognizable to the eye. Sometimes we use the term 'radiation' when we mean 'light', and vice versa. In fact visible 'light' is a form of radiation, For example, a radio wave is light with a wavelength of about one metre, or one million times larger than visible colour red. X-rays are light with wavelength about five thousand times shorter than blue. Gamma rays, have waves generated by radioactive atoms and nuclear explosions and these have the smallest wavelengths while they possess more energy than any other wave in the electromagnetic spectrum. When we put all the possible wavelengths together we call this the 'electromagnetic spectrum', and it is clear that the visible light is only a tiny part of it. Visible light has waves of the right length (between 750 to 400 nanometers) and frequency to be picked up by the cone cells of the eye while the invisible light do not have those qualities. This, at least, partly explains the state of the formless and dark earth.

What precedes leads to the following hypothesis: Invisible lights that have the longest waves and the lowest frequencies may be lacking in refraction and reflection and for that reason may carry the least amount of contained energy. For the reverse reason, the invisible lights of higher frequency may have higher refraction and reflection and carry a greater amount of contained energy. Dark matter and dark energy might each be relevant to either one or the other. It would follow that the difference between dark energy and dark matter simply a question of degree.

Without light, energy is non-dimensional and as far as reason and even science can tell, in this state, it must diffuse, uniformly in all directions without limit, a concept that surpasses exact knowledge and is beyond a phenomenon that we can understand. One thing that science can verify, though, is that dark energy is increasing in quantity at an accelerating rate. Even the Copernican principle, which states that there is no special place or special direction in the Universe, agrees with this observation.

The form of matter is perceived as light by the sense of sight and its energy is perceived as heat by the sense of touch. Degradation of matter from the **sun** is perceived as light by the eyes and as heat by the sense of touch. When the earth obstructs the eat and energy that escape separately for the sun we have night with its coolness and darkness. We find this also in fire. When something burns, it disintegrates releasing light and heat. Fire being light and heat, lead the early philosophers to similar conclusions: "Some held the firmament to be of the nature of the four elements, not, indeed, compounded of them, but being as it were a simple element. Such was the opinion of Plato, who held that element to be fire."[28]

The light and the energy (heat) coming from the disintegration of matter in the sun are captured by the vegetative soul and recompose and integrated to form the material part of plants. This, in turn becomes nourishment for the animal life.

Void does not have existence. In space (what we call space) there is energy without dimensional form. If it were not so we would not be able to see the celestial bodies since light cannot cross a void. Modern physical science hypothesizes that energy "permeates all of space" and calls it "dark energy". But if there is a pure energy that has no dimension, in what way can it be finite? We can only hypothesize that it is limited in a way similar to that of the pure spirits (angels, separate substances) which are dimensionless yet finite. The senses cannot perceive either one and nor the mind imagine them - their existence can only be known by abstraction or by experimental science. However, being dimensionless, energy does not necessarily

---

[28]Thomas Aquinas, Summa Theologica, Pt. 1, Q. 68, Art. 2

have to be infinite since it naturally tends towards union with the form where it acquires dimension and becomes limited. The result of such a marriage will be matter or prime matter. Therefore prime matter can be said to be energy married to its first form, that is, the quantitative form of light as was shown earlier. Likewise, *formless matter* is more exactly expressed as *formless energy*. God creates the essences of energy and form from his own Essence. The two are distinct from each other, yet become one essence when united to one another.

So, the formless and void Earth of the Book of Genesis can be understood as energy not yet united to the form of visible light. Once that union has occurred the resulting physical or sensible matter will be in acceptance of the individuating forms that will multiply it at different level. This evolution of creation will now be developed and can be outlined as follows:

- Energy + light = matter.
- Matter + soul = life.
- First soul = vegetative life.
- vegetative life + second soul = animal life.
- Animal life + intellect = human life.
- human life + divine participation = perfection of creation.
- Man: divine by participation
- Christ: divine in essence.

At this point, after having considered the earth, it might be relevant to go directly to the fourth day according to the biblical narration where it is written that God said "Let there be lights in the vault of heaven to divide day from night and let them indicate festivals, day and year." On earth the sun is master of light and energy. The light-energy feeds the plants that feeds the beasts and man during the day, but allows rest at night. This illustrates God's plan for the passage of time, from day to night, until the end. *Day and night* is what measures the flow of time and allows the recording of events according to the movement of heavenly bodies to which family the earth itself belongs. The divine plan unfolds day after day until the first and the last are united in the *final cause*). The days and the nights keep the tally of human history from its antecedent forms until that of eternal glory. On them recorded history rest.

Now going back to the third day, God said: "Let the water under the sky be gathered into a single basin, so that the dry land may appear." (...) Then God said, "Let the earth bring forth vegetation: every kind of plant that bears seed and every kind of fruit tree on earth that bears fruit with its seed in it". Thus, according to the biblical account the appearance of life on earth is also associated with that of water. Why does the Bible give such importance to water? In fact, water is full of mystery, both theologically and scientifically. Experimental science has only begun to explore, within its domain, the mystery of water. Oxygen is created by nuclear reactions in the stars. If H and O are married in the cold of space, H_2O results. There are enormous amounts of water in space. In fact, nearly all of the oxygen in space is in the form of water or carbon monoxide. Similarly, most the carbon and nitrogen in space are also in their hydrogenated forms: methane (CH_4) and ammonia (NH_3). Water adheres to carbon to form the carbohydrate that will support the vegetative soul. It is the support of life. (Life is the organizing cause of the vegetative soul. It organizes matter in such a way that it can grow and overcome gravity by nourishing itself. Furthermore, it can reproduce itself in different ways.)

It is true that science conveys the idea of *carbon-based* life forms and we must recognize that carbon has some very special chemical properties such as its ability to form strong and stable bonds capable of creating structures which will link up into the long chains that feature the molecules of life. If life is ever going to get started on any planet, carbon is surely needed, but even before that, life needs flowing water. Without water, life simply cannot be sustained. It is the fluid that lubricates the workings of the cell, transports the materials and molecular machinery from one place to another and facilitates the chemical reactions that perpetuates life. It is a sustenance and cleansing fluid, bearing nutrients to where they are needed and taking away wastes. It is even a structural agent in plants. Some cells can avoid death if their water is extracted, but then they shut down utterly until they are rehydrated. Without water, other biomolecules would not only be left stranded and immobile, they might no longer truly be biomolecules; they would unravel or seize up and lose their biological function in the process. Water plays an active role in the life of the cell, to the extent that we can consider it to be a kind of biomolecule. In scanning through the literature of modern molecular biology, one could be forgiven for concluding that the subject is all about proteins and genes, embodied in the nucleic acid DNA. But this is only a form of shorthand; for biology is really all about the interactions of such molecules in and with water. Water seems to be the medium of a new stage of creation, life's true and unique medium. It is the matrix of life.

The hypothesis that water is at the origin of life cannot be explained nor discredited by science. One must have recourse to theology or even philosophy to give it credit. However, the question of how life issues from H2O can receive inspiration from the Augustinian theory of *rationes seminales* according to which "continuing spontaneous generation is made possible by a divine decree issued at the moment of creation and active forevermore, under whose power the generation of living creatures from the earth and various organic materials persists."[29] Augustine referred to biblical commands such as: "Let the land produce living creatures according to their kinds."

---

[29]Frey, Iris, *The Emergence of Life on Earth,* Rutgers University Press, New Brunswick, 2000, p.17.

He said that the first event of creation was the formation of the "seed-principles" (*rationes seminales*) of all the species, which where the potentials of all living creatures to come. These potentials materialized throughout the history of the Earth according to a preordained plan when the conditions are favourable.[30] Such favourable conditions must include water, the "matrix of life"; its true and unique medium. Life does not exist by itself. As everything else in the order of Creation, life is founded on love and love necessitates an alter one. Accordingly, life is united to matter and joined together by water. Here, one finds the root of the idea of *rationes seminales,* which is, in essence, the theory of evolution originating with the Creator.

Since the idea of evolution appears and reappears in this essay, we should not bypass this opportunity to examine it from its biblio-philosophical perspective which includes a Cause moving things towards an end. Paleontology can testify to it although not with complete certitude. Human beings do not live long enough to witness it although some genetic adaptations may be observed particularly in primitive and simple life such as the microbic. Viewed from a philosophical perspective, the following biblical passage does tell us something about evolution: *"God fashioned man of dust from the soil. Then he breathed into his nostrils a breath of life, and thus man became a living being."[31]*. That dust becomes man through God's creative power implies a progressive development whereby forms are accumulated and diversified according to a design ordered to an end. At some point, along the process of becoming man, dust is no more dust

---

[30]Currently, microfossils within rocks dated from 3.77 to 4.28 billion years old found in Québec, Canada, may be the oldest record of life on Earth, suggesting "an almost instantaneous emergence of life" after ocean formation 4.4 billion years ago.

[31]Gen. 2; 7.

and yet not man. Time is continuous and so is the movement of matter which it measures; therefore, there is a continuity between dust and man which cannot be breached without nullifying the biblical affirmation. However, the Bible reveals that this becoming stops short of man as a spiritual being. That "ontological leap" happened when God breathed the breath of life into the creature He had fashioned to become an intellectual creature able to receive a spiritual existence. Man appeared on the last day of creation, but, "*with the Lord...* (according to the words of St. Peter) *a day can mean a thousand years, and a thousand years is like one day.*" We could say, as well, that with the Lord one day can he a thousand million years, since God is outside of time and not limited by it.

So, are we saying that Creation began before time? According to Augustine *(Gen. ad lit. i. 15; iv. 22, 34 ; De Gen. contr. Manich. i, 5, 7)*, the order of creation is not of duration, but only of origin and nature. He says that the formless spiritual and formless corporeal natures were created first of all, and that the latter are at first indicated by the words *earth* and *water*. This formlessness did not precede formation in time, but it did so only in origin; nor did one formation precede another in duration, but it did so merely in the order of nature. Agreeably, then, to this order, the formation of the highest or incorporal nature is recorded in the first place, where It is said that light was made on the first day. For as the spiritual nature is higher than the corporeal, so the higher bodies are nobler than the lower. Hence the formation of the higher bodies is indicated in the second place, by the words, *Let there be made a firmament*, by which is to be understood the impression of celestial forms on formless matter, that preceded with priority not in time, but of origin only. But in the third place the impression of elemental forms on formless matter is recorded, also with a priority of origin only. Therefore the words,

Let the waters be gathered together, and the dry land appear, mean that corporeal matter was impressed with the substantial form of water, so as to have such movement, and with the substantial form of earth, so as to have such an appearance.

One may wonder, given that the material world in its formless state is a limitless quantity of energy, if philosophical reasoning and biblical inspiration could not help experimental science to discover the invisible world of this virtual energy and by so doing gain accessibility to its infinite energy for the good of mankind. Science cannot gain complete knowledge without reference beyond the senses although the senses tell us that there has to be another world that is not tangible. The pot cannot know even itself without acknowledging the potter.

At the stage of creation beyond that of vegetative life, the animal soul appears when sensitivity and free mobility are added to the vegetative soul. These are complemented by a heart, needed to sustain the mobility, and a brain, needed to coordinate these new abilities. This new form of life which perfects that of the vegetative soul happens on the fifth day when God says: "*Let the water teem with living creature, and let birds fly above the earth within the vault of heaven*" Then the sixth day follows with a further development within that animal soul as the Creator pronounces his effective Word, " *Let the earth produce every king of living creature : cattle (...) and every kind of wild beast*", that is, mammals.

Life, at this new stage is a form that organizes and elevates the previous formation of energy to a superior state. However, it remains totally subjected to the material state. The life of the animal soul depend on the body's lifeblood, which is regarded as the seat of vitality. As long as the organ called "heart" circulates the lifeblood and distributes its vital elements throughout the whole body, the soul subsist, but as soon as it fail to do so the body dies and the soul disappears.

But there is intelligence, which from the beginning of creation was a property of the First Cause, and without it knowledge would come to a premature halt, leaving the essentals to a wasted end . It is also the *end cause* of creation, where the intellect emerges and allows unity with the One who is the *First and the Last* of creation. So God, who created the visible world out of Himself and out of nothing other than Himself, infused in it from the very beginning, an *end cause* that would gradually take it through a preordained and infused transformation, from *prime matter* to the totally subjugated soul of vegetative life, to the added sensitivity and mobility of the animal soul and finally to the added intellect of the human soul that gives it freedom of choice and allows it to participate in the spiritual life. While the animal life with its vegetative component sustains the human intellectual soul, it also constrains it. However, the intellect, being of a spiritual nature, will survive its physical host.

PART III

The divine government

We saw that God creates material essences by bringing them to existence, that is, by giving their forms (or ideas) an energy to marry[32] and thereby to multiply. In an analogous way, we can also say that man creates. In reality, man can only cause a *becoming* in a reality that is already existing and predetermined by a form, which is why art or any the human creation is limited by the nature of the object. The reason for this, is that God alone can communicate *being* because He alone has Being for essence. Creatures, by contrast, can exist only by participating of the Supreme Being, the self-existent One. Thus, according to Aquinas, one can say that "being is by itself consecutive to the form of the creature, as long as we posit the active intervention of God".[33] He compared this necessary intervention to the action of the sun by means of which the light becomes the consequence of the diaphaneity of the air. God is the First Cause of all that exists. The things he realizes carry a certain art, that of giving forms to a potentiality considered as energy. The model of this realization that we call creation is in divine wisdom. Since His essence is Being, God exercises his regency in an absolute manner, but His "active intervention" allows for the intermediate agencies of created intelligences .

So, what is divine government? The expression can be defined while establishing a distinction between it and the term divine providence. While *divine providence* can be defined concisely as "the reason for the *ordering* of things to their ends which preexist in the divine intelligence",[34] that of *divine government* implies an *act of the will*

---

[32]There is marriage between the energy of one form and the energy of another form.

[33]*Summa Theologica*, I, q. 104, s.1

[34]Emile Filion, *op. cit.*, p. 138.

directed to an end. Thus, there is a necessary immediacy between Providence and Creation, while government is done not only immediately but *mediately*. In other words, when divine government orders or directs people to the end that Providence has preconceived for their own good, it does so immediately by sustaining their lives and taking part in their operations, but also, it does so by means of the instrumental action of intermediaries. Through their activities, as secondary causes, created realities contribute to the establishment of order and the achievement of their own ends while remaining in total dependence on God. We call the idea that God has of this participation : *eternal law*. That He determines how he will provide for this, is called *providence*. That He gives effect to it in providing for its implementation, this is called *divine government*. It follows that providence is the main cause of eternal law, while divine government is its effect. Providence is therefore the central concept to which are attached (while distinguishing them) the notions of creation and government. Indeed, all this is the same thing, so when discoursing on divine government, the distinctions of priority, which were just briefly reviewed, will be taken for granted without referring to them anymore.

God governs the irrational *formed energy* (or *corporeal being*) through the intermediary of nature, i.e. by means of the determinations he has inscribed into it. Despite the contingencies that may deviate from the established order in nature, the divine government does not fail to bring all things to universal perfection and to its own glory. However, irrational things, such as "sounding cymbals" glorify God through the rational soul belonging to man. In this case, the the cymbal functions as instrument for man, while the latter has an intermediary function within the spiritual return of nature to its creator. Such is the teaching of Thomas Aquinas as demonstrated by in the following passage:

An effect can occur outside of the order created by a particular cause, but not outside the order created by a universal cause. The reason of this is that no effect results outside the order of a particular cause, except through some other impeding cause; which other cause must itself be reduced to the first universal cause; as indigestion may occur outside the order of the nutritive power by some such impediment as the coarseness of the food, which again is to be ascribed to some other cause, and so on till we come to the first universal cause. Therefore as God is the first universal cause, not of one genus only, but of all being in general, it is impossible for anything to occur outside the order of the Divine government; but from the very fact that from one point of view something seems to evade the order of Divine providence considered in regard to one particular cause, it must necessarily come back to that order as regards some other cause.[35]

When it comes to God, the preconceived end in His mind includes the *raison d'être* of each of his creatures. According to Émile Filion, the divine government is the "virtual effect of divine providence which consists in that creatures tend towards the end willed by God, according to the ordination of this providence[36]." Creation can be seen *in God* as being *ab aeterno* but this may not be the case for the divine government, since it involves a movement that draws the creatures to an end determined by their author, therefore something temporal. This does not imply a new relationship between God and the world, but the same relationship under different modes. In the case of creation *ab aeterno* there is simply a relationship of reason between the creator and creatures, as multiplicity and movement does not exist in God. On the other hand, the relationship is true in the case of

---

[35] *Summa Theologica*, I, q. 103 a.7
[36] Emile Filion, *op. cit.*, p. 151.

the governed world, since there is a real distinction between the agent who moves and the object being moved.

At this point, I believe it is important in this context to quote Emile Filion's explanation (op. *cit.*, p. 144.) of Creation as immanent operation: "No operation formally transitive can really be appropriate for God; indeed an immanent operation is an operation that has its beginning and end in the operating subject, therefore it is from the very perfection of this agent, and it is subjectively independent of any extrinsic principle; however, the transitive operation is an operation that has its principle in the subject, but has its term outside the subject; accordingly transitive operation tends first to the perfection of the patient, which it requires absolutely. But God tends first to his own essential perfection; His operation cannot depend on an extrinsic principle; He is the subsistent Being; He is Being in itself, therefore he is his own operation and he operates from Himself independently of any extrinsic principle therefore all of God's operations are strictly immanent."

Divine government is exercised for a double effect: to keep the corporeal beings in existence, first by leading them to their ultimate end,[37] namely God himself, then to govern them towards the good that emerges from their general perfection and perfect bliss of the rational life in the formed energies of man. Since goodness is the reason for the end, the supreme good emerges from the ultimate end. When the divine government leads the creatures towards the good of intermediate ends, it is for the highest good of the ultimate end. This double aspect is outlined in this author's work on the *Ontological Foundation of Regency*.[38]

---

[37]From the divine perspective, this end is the extrinsic glorification of God.
[38]See *Appendix B.*

God acts in two ways to keep the material energy in its forms and keep the realized corporeal being in existence. In the first way, the act of preservation is perceived negatively and it consists of discarding any element that could corrupt the corporeal being by lowering it from a higher integrated form to lower multiple forms. (Ex. The living body decays into single compounds or elements after losing his animated form.) In such a case, the act of preservation is done from the outside. (E.g. salt eliminates decomposers, i.e. bacteria.) Since we were referring to material composition, we can deduce immediately that intangible corporeal being does not fall under this influence and that God does not have to intervene this way to preserve their formation.

In the second way we perceive the act of conservation positively. This is a direct action to keep the real things in existence. Without this act of divine volition, matter would lose its original form and return to non-commensurability. In the De Potentia,[39] Aquinas shows that conservation, in the existence of created things, depends on God, because any effect depends on the agent since it is the cause of that effect. This assertion is provable for each case, since each of them is essential to real existence. That one of them be subtracted and the thing which depends on it for existence will cease to exist as a reality. We saw, for example, that the substantial principles, energy and form, are essential for the formation of material substances. The same applies to the need for an efficient cause, because it gives energy its original form and, in the case of material substances, it causes complex matter to pass from one form to another. The final cause, for its part, is the intention of the agent without which it cannot move .

Concerning efficient causes, a distinction must be made between the one that "gives energy its original form" and the univocal agents

---

[39]Thomas Aquinas, *De Potentia*, q. 5, a.1 .

which are not by themselves direct causes of the material form. These agents produce effects of their own species and similar to themselves. This is explained by Thomas Aquinas in the following passage :

> Now, it is clear that of two things in the same species one cannot directly cause the other's form as such, since it would then be the cause of its own form, which is essentially the same as the form of the other; but it can be the cause of this form for as much as it is in matter - in other words, it may be the cause that *this matter* receives *this form*. And this is to be the cause of *becoming*, as when man begets man, and fire causes fire. Thus whenever a natural effect is such that it has an aptitude to receive from its active cause an impression specifically the same as in that active cause, then the *becoming* of the effect, but not its being, depends on the agent.[40]

To arrive at the cause proper to any transformation of matter, it will be necessary to go back to an supreme principle that can produce it by itself. The principle that gives energy its form must be incorporeal since the form on its own is immutable, while the bodies act only as they are moved and can move only things that are in potentiality, that is to say, in motion. This does not mean that there is no corporeal principles involved in the various embodiments of forms, but only in as much as they are instruments of the incorporeal principle. "Quantity does not altogether prevent the corporeal form from acting," wrote Thomas Aquinas", it prevents it from being an universal agent, in as much as the form is indivisible and linked to a matter subjected to quantity. (...) Such a body is inferior to such another in as much as it is in potentiality toward that which the other possesses in actuality." Above all, the function of the corporeal principles is to

---

[40] *Summa Theologica*, I, q. 104, a. 1

accommodate the energy to the form, because the latter requires a disposition that suits it. As energy acquires the forms that make it a material object it acquires at the same time determinations that restrict the degree of availability to other forms. The more forms the latest material object received from earlier compositions, the more limited will be the choices of compatible forms available. If there is this sort of immediate incompatibility, it falls upon the corporeal principle to transmute the corporeal being by giving it the accidents which will allow the form to accommodate itself to it – e.g. the green wood which is dried in order to allow its combustion. The corporeal principle will then act by virtue of the incorporeal principle, without which there would be no achieved forms or forms to achieved. On the other hand, its action will then be determined by the specific form which it possesses as a univocal agent. Thus, the man who fathers a child gives to the elements the necessary dispositions required to receive the form of another man, but the spiritual form which belongs to the species does not depend on him.

Corporeal agents thus contribute to the achievement of things, in as much as the power they hold from the principle predetermined by the substantial form allows them. That is to say, they have the power to educe the form of a material object and cause its *becoming* by marrying it to another material object. The reality and the being of this last result depend only indirectly on corporeal agents, which is why the *becoming* of what they produce ceases only when their action ends without, for all that, ending the being of the thing. Thus, the author of this thesis can disappear without causing the thesis itself to disappear, since he is no more the cause of its becoming. Yet the forms he built into a work were educed from the realities of the universe by multiple generations of predecessors.

According to the proposed theory, God keeps things in existence by maintaining spiritual energy in its first level of specification (separate substance) and its secondary and perfective degree of specification (corporeal substance in its evolutionary ascent). Conservation therefore requires a divine impulse, in the guise of a volitional and effective act. Man can reduce the forms of energy until the last, that is to say, that of the last quantitative energy that can be released from the atom. Then, the colour, the outer form, and other formal aspects will not exist any more in the atom. If it is fissioned further there will still some last form i.e. the measurability of energetic intensity. Should this final form be removed from matter, it would no longer exists in reality – by loosing its measurability it would also lose its reality - as it is the extension that makes a body what it is. In itself, the idea which is the form, has for function to define or particularize that which in God is infinite power. Absolute infinity and unity are inconceivable from the point of view of reality, since the latter is always perceived as multiplicity and finitude.

God is the only principle-agent who can inform energy and maintain in existence the material object resulting from this information. He alone can be the author of the specific form with which a substance is created. It is only in a metaphorical way that we can say that man creates. Therefore, his power is exercised only on the *becoming* of corporeal objects and, moreover, he can only lead them to their end while respecting the order that their Creator has established in their natures .

In concrete realities, real things appear under the influence of the principle agent as an energy enclosed in a quantitative form capable of receiving qualitative compositions. (E.g., light waves of different length giving different colors.) These compositions are accidental provisions that are transformable by man acting as a secondary agent. The action of the latter has the ability to effect the disappearance of a substantial form and replace it with another, but for doing so he needs a compatible material.

Man cannot avoid using already existing forms in nature and that even in the pure creativity of art and poetry. All the techniques that man uses can only bring bring him back to a stubborn naturalism as demonstrated by Jacques Maritain whom I quote here at length:

> What matters to us is that there are other painters, who really count in the movement of creative research, and who keep on being intent on doing a work, and being intent on beauty. These painters have been confronted with a growing difficulty inseparable from the advance of modern painting: namely the fact that, in proportion as the creativity of the spirit strives for greater and greater liberation in order for the Self to be revealed in the work, Nature discloses greater obstacles, or rather demands from poetic intuition a ceaselessly growing power, in order for things to be grasped, and expressed in the work, without hampering or thwarting the simultaneous expression of subjectivity and the freedom of the creative spirit. What was twenty years ago an invaluable conquest over naturalism will seem now still tainted with naturalism. Any representation whatever of natural appearances is seen as an obstacle to the free creativity of the spirit. And it is, in actual fact, as long as it has not yet been purified and transfigured in the pungent night of creative intuition. The road of creative intuition, however, is exacting and solitary, it is the road to the unknown, it passes through the sufferings of the spirit. Artists are always tempted to prefer the road of technical discoveries. (…)

> While dislocating natural appearances, neither Cubism nor Futurism did actually break with them. They tried to bring out from them a new visual significance – but by making this effort only with respect to external sensibility, and by relying finally on the discovery of a new technique, new tricks and means. (…)

There was, for a few years, another school. (...) I take it here as an instance of a possible theory, which it is, of philosophical interest to disengage in its generality. I imagine that, from this point of view, we might express this attempt at integral transmutation in the following way:

The painter looks at Things, at the universe of visible Being – intent to grasp in it some reality beyond appearances and some hidden meaning. He receives the poetic spark (even though charged perhaps with a somewhat sadistic electricity). Then he sets out to express what he has grasped, not by simply transposing the natural appearances of the objects involved, but by using the totally different appearances of other objects belonging in a totally separate sphere – without any flash of intuitive similarity springing forth between these distant objects: so that the secret reality grasped in Being will be expressed enigmatically, through a totally new creation totally contrived by his own spirit. A bride will become an insidious machine whose anatomy displays an ironical and icy complication of cylinders, pipes, and bevel gears.

Natural appearances will be totally transmuted into forms which pertain to another world of objects. The painter is an alchemist. He transmutes lead into gold, or gold into lead, kings, queens, and nudes into the volumes and surfaces of imaginary engines in motion, through which the ambiguous reality intended by him and the successive moments of this manifestation in time and movement are spread out in space. (..)

Creative intuition and imagination do not proceed in an angelic or demonic manner. They are human, bound to the alertness of sense perception. They grasp a certain transparent reality through the instrumentality of the eye and of certain natural appearance – they cannot express or manifest it except through the instrumentality of these same natural appearances, recreated, recast, transposed of course, not cast aside and totally replaced by other appearances proper to another realm of Things in the world of sensible Being. It's as good as having the soul of a flower in an elephant. In genuine metaphor, the illuminating image arrives from another world, as a bird through the window of your room, to quicken the transposition of natural appearances and their power of significance: it supersedes them only for an instant, it does not suppress them. Here, on the contrary, there is no illumination, nor illuminating image. The Thing within which creative intuition has caught its diamond is not illuminated, it is killed. The other Thing which has been conjured up does not suggest it, it absorbs it, and expresses it only in secret cipher. The process cuts off in human art the intellect from its inescapable connection with sense perception. It is unnatural in itself.[41]

As agent body, man cannot create his art beyond his power to transform the material cause of substances, that is to say, energy already in form. He accomplishes this transformation by extracting the form of a material substance. In fact, he extracts the form of a thing[42] which he then introduces in another substance capable of receiving it. For example, the artist who educes Plato's form from a block of marble, and the cabinetmaker the form of the wooden table, merely introduce into the material – by making it apt to receive them – the forms they had extracted. Because they are only indirectly the cause

---

[41]Maritain, Jacques, *Creative Intuition in Art and Poetry*, Meridian Books, New York, 1955, p.154-156.

[42]Essentially, man does not invent new forms, regardless of their complexity and originality, because all the possible forms already exists, at least potentially, if not actually.

of the reality produced, the latter, as has been said, continues to exist after the departure of the corporeal creator or agent. The corporeal agent causes the becoming of a thing, but not its being. Therefore, when the human creator ceases his causal action, the becoming of the reality he produced stops, but its being continues to exist.

On the other hand, because their becoming is not subjected to the movement inherent to matter, the incorporeal substantial cause will be the Incorporeal Agent who participates his Being to them for their becoming. As soon as the action of this Agent ceases, the realities produced by Him will also cease, because He is the only producer of forms and it is form alone that can give reality to the potentiality of energy and allow it to exist in its specificity. Once the Incorporeal Agent unites a form to the potentiality of energy, the resulting composite exists as a single substance. "He who gives form gives being," says Thomas Aquinas. This discourse affirms that God, supreme Incorporeal Agent, is the producer and preserver of substantial forms to which the name substance is here given.

How to differentiate the part of man from that of God in the production and preservation of things? While answering this question it will be necessary to take into account the different meanings that the word "being" can take. The operation of secondary causes, as we have seen, produces changes by the transmission of a form in a material object as subject. When the production of a thing is done by transformation, it can only be in an existing subject that is in potentiality for a relative change. We already know that the realization of prime matter surpasses the capability of a corporeal agent, therefore the capability of man, since the energy and the form of which it is comprised are only *a priori*, only in *virtual existence* in the Incorporeal Agent and only He can bring them to their common and real existence. On the other hand, at its prime formation, matter is the support of all corporeal substances while it is itself being supported by nothing other than the incorporeal Agent..

But man, as a secondary agent, can nevertheless produce an effect on a material substance and bring out a new form from material potentiality in order to substitute it for another form. The substituted form of matter so transformed returns to the virtual and universal potentiality, that is to say, to actual non-existence. We saw that man disposes the physical reality to receive a new form by acting on accidental qualities of the substance he wants to transform. It was said, moreover, that this is how the created agent produces the becoming of a form and takes part in its introduction into being. Also, it was seen that by using the determinations of material potentiality man causes the emergence of new forms of matter, without being the author of their being. For example, using materials appropriate to the construction of a bridge, the engineer is the author of the becoming of the bridge, but not the author of the formal determinations which already make up the material. By measuring the static energy determined by their forms the engineer can make an appropriate use of materials that give the bridge its stability. To get to the source of this stability, one must go back to the author of the marriage of form of energy, which cannot be, as we know, other than the Incorporeal Supreme Agent .

So, what we can say of man is that he contributes in a limited way to the determination of a thing by producing the becoming of the form. Since the latter is realized in matter, its becoming is also the becoming of the thing, and that is why we can say that man is the cause of its appearance. Man creates the thing in its becoming by causing it to be born in a new concrete nature - in a new essence – without, for that matter, making the information of the energy depend on him. As such, he neither causes the being of the thing nor does he causes its conservation.

Man, then, cannot be the cause of existence in as much as it is the material realization of the essence. He can produce an effect in as much as he has before him an informed energy apt at having its latest form exchanged for another for which it is in potentiality. When this transformation is realized, there is preservation of existence, which depends only on God. In the transition from one form to another, there is no annihilation: existence precludes any form. In support of this assertion, Charles-V. Héris writes:

> The existence, as such, that is to say, in as much as it is the ultimate act of a reality (*esse existantiae*) does not, in its production, come in any way under the created agent. The latter, indeed, may be the cause only as much as he has before him a subject in potentiality, at once deprived of the form to be produced and vested in a contrary form that has to be eliminated. But, existence, as such, *sic ut esse*, has no positive form that is contrary to it and which would constitute a deprivation for the being vested in it. Existence is opposed to outright non-being, to nothingness. It cannot be the effect of transmutation, it is the effect of pure efficiency. And He alone, Who has Being in itself, who is Existence itself, *Ipsum Esse subsistens*, can make other beings exist by creation. Thus, only He can conserve in being. Hence the conclusion of Thomas Aquinas: If God did not keep all things in existence, they would immediately go back to the nothingness from which they are drawn.[43]

---

[43]Héris, Ch -V, op. cit., p. 261.

We must not imagine that, in creating, God first gives being to a material energy, that He then realizes the being of the form, and finally composes the two beings into one corporeal substance. So in reality, there is only the outright existence of corporeal being with all its elements. The corporeal substances do not reach their reality of informed energy before existence be given to them by a cause independent of another cause. This is why, in the operations carried out by agents who do not have their own cause, we must admit a divine activity that produces and conserves the corporeal being. It falls to Him who is the cause of all existence to realize a reality according to different natures or essences subject to change, into which man insert himself as a participant. By subjecting to himself, while respecting them, the various determinations of these natures, the secondary human activities become productive so that man contributes to the divine activity. *In virtute Dei* affirms Thomas Aquinas, created causes (among them, man, created cause *per excellence*) act as instruments in the production of the becoming of corporeal reality .

We need to see, at this stage, where to situate idea of conservation of corporeal being in relation to the creation theory developed earlier. Does it consist of a continuous operation on the part of the First Cause who creates the multiple and motion by imposing determinations in His own virtual energy? If this is the case, can we establish a distinction in the operation? It was intimated that by imposing forms in his virtual energy the First Cause, God, introduces motion in his work and a certain continuity of action which necessarily involves time. So how can the information of the virtual energy of an extra-temporal Creator be achieved temporally?

The answer must begin with the idea of Creation as a becoming. The Infinite One introduces becoming[44] into His eternal present without producing any change in Himself since it is Being in itself which nothing can diminish or move. Viewed from our side, Creation is a becoming that is born from the *nothingness* of the virtual form and the unrealized energy. "Creation actively taken" Sertillanges writes, "is God's work drawing the world out of nothingness; passively taken, it is its coming out of this nothing and of its cause which we attribute to the universe in its first becoming. Therefore, we will not say anything more, referring ourselves to the furtherest down the ages : God creates the world, or: The world is actually created; our definition of words forbids it."[45] Consequently, there is, according to our understanding, a beginning and something new that is introduced in Being under the aspect of duration, but on the side of its author, so to speak, becoming is neither movement nor time .

Analogously, in the absence of its becoming, Creation is only a divine species which the form encompasses without absorbing it. That is to say, it is the eternal idea, at once virtually universal and manifold, which is contained in the energetic potentiality deprived of the temporal reality that its union to the form would make appear. By uniting itself to energy in the aspect of a form, the idea gives birth to the first becoming which we conceive as Creation, and the corporeal being thus created is born and made aware of its intelligibility by the consciousness and intelligence of its human part. The intelligence embodied with its introduction into matter is designed with all of Creation as a duration which pursues its perfection in becoming. Thus, because of this becoming, Creation differs specifically from conservation. Generically the latter is prior to creation because of the timelessness of God's government of which it is the effect. In other words, conservation is an aspect of the eternal present, prior to creation, but an aspect that is plunged into the temporality or duration

---

[44]It is idea of a transition from the virtual to reality.

[45]Sertillanges, Antonin. -D., *La philosophie de S. Thomas d'Aquin*, Editions Montaigne, Paris, 1940, Volume I, p. 265. Trans. J.-N. Chabot.

of motion. In God, as in thought, the idea of the beginning and the end subsists permanently .

However, in its deepest reality, Creation is not, itself, a becoming. As a specific difference, becoming expresses only a part of the idea of Creation: that of change. In relation to its genus, Creation is eternal conservation, that is to say, in order to continue to be, it has to maintain a relation of dependence on its Creator, because it exists only by participating in him. Charles-V. Héris says it well:

> As creation is a relationship, nothing stands in its permanence: it suffices that it be established to last the duration of its foundation in face of its end, in other words the duration of the universe.

He then adds :

> From this real point of view, conservation is not anything other than the creation itself, once posited, it remains. Hence the term continuous creation, often used to define conservation.[46]

Obviously, from the side of God, creation implies neither time nor motion. We cannot identify, in any way whatsoever, the First Cause - which has in itself the power and the exercise of this power – with the created causes, which exercise in different ways, in dependence on this First Cause, the act of conservation. Sertillanges takes note of it in the following passage:

> Properly, *to continue*, is to act over time. If God is outside of time, what is right is not to say that He continues, himself, to give being to the world, but that the world itself continues the evolution of its being. God is the reason why the world is and is

---

[46]Héris , Ch-V, op. cit., p. 263. Trans. J-N. Chabot

always; God is not the cause, always, that the world is. Although we may write it indifferently to the active and passive case, by reason of the logical correlation of which S. Thomas noted the use, this verb to conserve should be understood only in the passive case because we now know and should not forget, that under any circumstances, between God and creatures relationships go up and do not come down.

God is the first cause, so He is the cause of being as being, therefore He is the cause of all that is according to all what it is, therefore also according to its measures, and therefore also according to its temporal extension as according to its spatial extension, as according to its essence: such, here, is the file of ideas, such is the condition we mean to express when we say God conserves the world.

It follows that duration being in such a manner united to the solid objects it measures, in as much as they are in causal relationship with God, that relationship is considered in itself extra temporal. Time could dominate only if it enveloped the two terms. Since one of them escapes it, and the other takes it, that is time, to integrate the whole object which is to be referred to God, so it is that this *ongoing* relationship we're talking about is in itself neither continuous nor non-continuous, but outside of all time measurement. Only its created foundation lasts and continues to be; duration itself does not last, does not continue, it is, and by it the world lasts, suspended to God according to its duration as according all the rest.[47]

When we look at the question of conservation of creatures by God directly or indirectly maintained with the participation of created

---

[47]Sertillanges, Antonin. -D., *La philosophie de S. Thomas d'Aquin*, Editions Montaigne, Paris, 1940, Volume I, p. 268.

causes, we must distinguish between its negative or positive understanding. If conservation is negatively understood, it will mean the elimination of the agents of corruption. In this case, the material causes that contribute to the conservation of the creatures will be many and in this there is no problem.

The real issue arises in relation to the positive conservation of creatures in their being, that is to say, when God acts as the ultimate first cause. It belongs to God alone to conserve the corporeal beings, which he does by allowing them to participate in his own Being. As the effect of the intermediate cause is to produce the becoming of things, it would follow, it seems, that once the production is completed, it would only have to disappear with its *raison d'être*. Its existence could only be maintained by God, the proper cause of every being. But there lies not the solution, as we can see, the conservation of corporeal beings is perfected in Creation by these intermediate causes which are subordinate to one another. Not that the First Cause is not the ultimate principle of conservation, but it is for the lower causes to contribute according to their ordination in relation to their proximity to the First Cause .

The acquisition of forms when they depend on the created cause is always produced by a change that occurs on a subject. However, once the change has occurred, the same cause which is its author may very well conserve it without any no new mutation. When I trigger a switch, a change occurs and the room in which I find myself lights up. Thereafter, the light bulb continues to illuminate the same space without an additional mutation being required. Of course, the created agent because it possesses only a secondary efficient cause cannot be the author of the form as such; no more than I can be the author of the energy that is transformed into light in the light bulb. Only God, as First Cause, can be the proper cause, the *ipse dator formarum*, of the form. Aquinas gives this question the following clarification :

The action of a corporeal agent does not extend beyond movement, and that is why it is the instrument of the First Agent in the passage of forms from potentiality to actuality, which is done by means of motion. But it is not the same for the conservation of forms, if not that, through a certain motion, the appropriate dispositions for such a form are maintained in matter. Thus, through the movement of celestial bodies, the lower realities are kept in being.[48]

Therefore, that mode of participation, by which man can contribute to the conservation of a new reality, consists in acting on matter in such a way that it will retain the dispositions which allowed the form to realize this new corporeal being when, as a created cause, he moved it from potentiality to actuality. Matter, since it always has a tendency to take on other dispositions, must be kept as it is in its new reality by having recourse to the motion that has educed the form from it by passing from potentiality to act. For example, the power that brought the tungsten bulb to the degree of heat required for its incandescence continues its efforts to maintain the element at the same degree of heat. Thus, there is analogy between the continuous generation by creatures who, as secondary causes, produce the becoming of things, and the continuous Creation by God who, as First Cause, keeps the completed corporeal being in participation of his Infinite Being.

When by the marriage of form and energy God introduces motion and the multiple in His infinite being, there is immediate creation. That God alone creates from Himself does not mean he does not conserve what he created without intermediaries. But in this respect, there are two species of corporeal beings to be distinguished. In the porphyry

---

[48]Summa Theologica, I, q.5, a.1 ad 7.

tree the corporeal is the difference between material substances and immaterial substances. There are, therefore, at the highest degree of universality, corporeal substances and incorporeal substances. If Thomas Aquinas argues for the necessary existence of incorporeal substances we can at least take it as a hypothesis and place it logically in the orders of *formed energy* and of *formed spirit (Angel)*.[49]

So, we can consider the existence of the angel in a way similar to the existence of the human intellectual soul because both can subsist by themselves. Because of their immateriality, these species cannot be produced otherwise than immediately. On the other hand, the types that are only corporeal are born by begetting. They were, nevertheless, created in the beginning when there was nothing that could engender them. However, the order of the universe reveals that its author, having completed its work immediately, desired to give it greater perfection by making it participate in His causality in addition to His Being. Among created things, there is an order of dependence according to which certain things receive from a secondary cause that part of their being which is due to their becoming. Thus, upon their realization, the unity of form and energy would be preserved by intermediaries.

However, the fact that a created cause is able to conserve its effect does not mean that it can maintain its own existence. Since the causal being which begets another cannot produce itself, it follows that the conservation of which he is the cause is nothing more than a continued generation.

God is not only the first cause of conservation, but in their proper activity the corporeal beings also depend on Him for their operation. It is suitable only for the Creator to produce potentialities that are

---

[49]Thomas Aquinas believed that reason must postulate them : (Summa Theologica, I, q. 14, a. 8 & I, q 19, a. 4)

principles of the operations of the will and intelligence. God is the condition of the reasonable and free being's operation: such is the case of man when he tends towards his own good without, for that, constituting the main cause in the proper sense. Doubtless God, as First Cause, can educe new forms from matter and produce, immediately, any particular effect or any accidental effect without the help of nature, but a perfection results from the active participation of the material and spiritual creatures of the universe. It must be concluded, on behalf of common sense, that having given the creatures an operating power derived from their forms, their Creator wanted them to use it. How can we make sense of the existence of free corporeal beings if they could not act for their perfections, that is to say, for their end?

It remains to be seen, what is the hand of God in the natural and voluntary operation of creatures. Excluded from this question, will be the production of the very existence of the effect, which belongs only to God, as we have already seen. Although the operation is the cause of an effect it will be question here only of the proper activity itself.

To come to know God's part in the operations of corporeal beings, it is useful to refer to causes that are not indeterminate, that is to say, those moved by the final cause, the agent and the form. Matter, as subject of an action is pure passivity. That's why it does not come into play when it comes to sharing in the operation of corporeal beings .

The final cause, because it acts as a term, virtually contains the others in itself. Being extrinsic, it differs from the efficient cause in that it moves by attraction; thus, corporeal beings always act for an end which appears to them as a good. Plato had a reason to believe that there is but one sovereign Good; the other goods are only participation in that one. Whether they have the real notion of it or only its appearance, what humans in appetite of the good pursue definitely is none other than the Supreme Good. Even the corporeal beings who do not have the faculty of intelligence tend towards God - whom the Sovereign Good represents - when they obey the appetite that leads them to the particular goods that are auxiliaries of their perfection. So it is that the whole world yearns for union with its first efficient Cause, by whom it comes into existence and to whom the becoming returns it. Its whole activity is an attraction to its source, to the Being in whom it participates. Aristotle expressed it well by saying that "the world hangs on to God by its desire ."

As a first efficient cause, God is the source of all the created activities, whether they proceed from nature or from the will. In the most general sense, activity is a movement that occurs when there is passage from potency to act. We saw that in the context of a demonstration of the existence of God that the existence of a first uncaused Cause is necessary absolutely. There is a corollary of this demonstration which applies to movement, which is that explaining the latter requires a prime mover that is moved by no other. So, there is no created activity that does not depend on God for its first movement. Thus we can say, with Aquinas, that "any application of a potentiality to its operation comes principally from God." The Aquinas explains as follows :

> The operative virtues are indeed applied to their own operations by a movement of either the body or the soul; however, the first principle of the one and the other movement is God because he is the prime mover altogether immobile. And similarly any movement of the will, by which the potentialities are to be applied to act, goes back to God as the first mover of the appetite and of the will. All operations must be attributed to God as the first and principal agent.[50]

---

[50]Thomas Aquinas, *Summa against the Gentiles*, Bk. III, ch. 67.

When we consider the form as a principle of action, we can say of it
what we have said of the efficient cause. This principle depends, in its
turn, on the divine operation which works as the first active ingredient.
We can consider this dependence in three ways: First, the movement
that the activity of the second causes take from their own form, is
received from the First Cause, that is to say from God who endows it
with active potentiality. The first five sections of *The Book of Causes*
assert this principle. They are as follows :

a) A First Cause produces its effect more than does the second
universal cause.

b) So, when the second universal cause removes its power
from one thing, the first universal cause does not deprive it of its
own power.

c) The reason is that the first universal cause acts on the effect
of the second cause, even before the latter, which accompanies
the former, acts on it.

d) When, therefore, the second cause, which accompanies the
effect, acts, its action does not escape that which is above it.

e) And when the second cause, which accompanies the effect,
is separated from it, the first cause, which is above the second
cause, is not separated from it, because it is the cause of it.

God therefore gives an active potentiality of their own directly to the
free corporeal beings, while he gives it to the predetermined corporeal
beings by means of the created causes.[51] Finally, since nothing
subsists without continuous intervention of the Supreme Cause, all
these forms or active potentialities are conserved by God.

God moves predetermined things in virtue of the determinations he
inscribed in nature when informing matter. These determinations are
also shared by man, but in him there is a part which is not

---

[51]The intellectual soul is not the product of matter, as we have seen.

predetermined; that is, the immaterial part or the intellect, which makes the will free. Let's just say that God moves corporeal beings through the intermediary of formal determinations, that is to say, according to the active potentialities of their natures. Man also acts according to a certain formal determination, as far as it determines the energy of his corporeal being. It was seen that man is also predetermined towards the good where the only freedom that comes to him is the choice between immediate goods.

That the role of God in the activity of creatures as was just described does not detract from the proper activity of the secondary cause. Despite the fact that the form on which depends the act can only communicate the potentiality to act and must obtain the support of a being in actuality to take action, the corporeal being still retain the property of their acts. As the first agent, God operates at a level other than the corporeal being which He causes to act as a second agent, but the activity is nonetheless produced under the effect of the two causes. It is truly the teacher who is the cause of the writing on the board, but it remains that the writing is the proper action of chalk. As Thomas Aquinas said, "God gives every creature forms that are principles of their activity; He conserves them in being, He applies them to acts, He is finally, himself, the final cause of every action."[52]

We cannot avoid the difficulty that arises regarding the role of God in the activity of the intellectual corporeal being whose actions are not predetermined but free. In the case of man, the freedom proper to the intellect is limited by the material determinations, while it remains free regarding the voluntary choice in accord with its form. Intrinsic to its substantial composition, and principle of its activity, the form or the soul of man operates immanently. Its activity begins with itself and is found within itself once it has reached its end. Thus, is the voluntary activity exercised. But, it must be remembered that even if he is free,

---

[52]Summa Theologica, I, q. 105, a.5, ad 3.

man receives from God the potentiality of his will and the application of this potentiality to his action since the First Cause is the principle of any voluntary act. This leads us to ask what is the contribution of the voluntary secondary cause in the act and its effect. Thomas Aquinas writes, in the following quotation from the *Summa Contra Gentiles*, that the contribution proper to the free agent in the production of a corporeal being is the determination of the act :

> The order of effects is correlative to the order of causes. So, what is first in the order of effects, is being «esse» because everything else is determination of being. The proper effect of the first agent is, therefore, being, and all the other agents produce it only by virtue (or power) of the first agent. The secondary agents, who particularize somehow and determine the action of the first agent, have for proper effect the other perfections or determinations of being.[53]

So, it is as moved by the divine action that man determines by his own voluntary power how to accomplish the effect of his act. Human action cannot, therefore, be achieved by itself, since God is its principle. This is, furthermore, affirmed by Aquinas:

> It is said that the will is master of his act, not by excluding the first cause, but in the sense that the first cause does not act on the will to the point of determining a single act, as it determines Nature. That is why the determination of the act remains in the power of reason and the will.[54]

From the fact that He is the principle, we deduce that God is himself the distant cause of the willed and executed action of man, but only

---

[53]Thomas Aquinas, *Summa Contra Gentiles*, III, ch. 66.
[54]*Thomas Aquinas, De Potentia*, q. 3, a. 7, ad 13.

for what there is of perfection in the determinations because there is no deprivation of being in God. The part of non-being in these determinations rests solely with human participation. The following is a follow-up to the previous quotation:

> Because the First Cause has more influence on the effect that the secondary cause, all that that there is of perfection in the effect relates (reductur) mainly to the First Cause; what is defective, on the contrary, must relate to the secondary cause which does not act as effectively as the First Cause.[55]

We know, of course, when we say that God is the First Cause in the act of the human will we do not mean that this is a question of priority of time, but a priority of nature. Since each corporeal being exist by participating of God, the Absolute Being, the latter is most intimately present in each created activity, as much in that which belongs to a predetermined nature as that which belongs to a free and intelligent nature. This is why we say that when man acts by participating in the divine activity, it is through God that he acts. In this, man is free, so much freer because he participates in the very freedom of the One who gives him existence. The divine action at the heart of the human will does not entail any violence or coercion, as is affirmed by Thomas Aquinas when he writes that "any cause whatsoever, does not exclude freedom, but only the cause which exerts violence, and it is not in that manner, that God is the cause of our operation."

We inferred that any movement from potentiality to act requires the causality of the First Mover. According to this consideration, we acknowledge two dispositions in relation to the will: Whether, in general, it is in potentiality to will or in potentiality to individual acts of the will. We can also consider the will according to its nature or

---

[55]*Ibid.*, ad 14.

according to its freedom, but remembering, in doing so, that any movement of the spirit must aim at the universal good, by means of the concrete and particular goods accessible to it. What moves things, is not the universal that one abstract from a particular good, but the latter itself. However, as a participant in the universal good, the particular good has by itself the capability to move affection beyond itself. Thus, the will awakens to the good as such. The affection that moves the will in this way carries within itself a double distinction whose aspects overlap. In the first instance, it is predetermined and moves the will by its nature, toward the pure and simple universal good, while in the second instance, it is indeterminate and moves the will freely towards the individual good.

So we see that at its principle the *formed energy* receives a finality that comes from the voluntary potentiality tending towards actuality. This actualization comes from God, because it is the property of the divine goodness to move the creatures towards the good in itself through the particular goods. Thus, voluntary potentiality is the effect of the divine act which makes it able to perform the *reversion* of matter to the spirit so that it is God himself who leads its creation to its ultimate good. In reality, however, at first the will only perceives the concrete attraction and it follows that before any reflection, the divine influence seems to disappear with the thrust of the affectivity in potentiality of a concrete good. However, with the awareness that operates by virtue of its disposition to reflect, the free will, while perceiving the limit and the relativity of particular goods that attract it, freely determines to choose between the concrete goods that offer themselves to it .

So, it can only be attributed to God that the good alone can have a relationship, with the appetite acting through it, on the will which is in potentiality to a choice. It remains to be seen whether this movement, acting on emotions, suffices by itself to allow the will to choose freely the particular good that suits it. There are solid reasons not to believe it and I agree with the argument of Charles V. Héris that follows:

> When a created causality is in actuality, it means that it is immediately applied to produce a given effect and is acting to achieve it. In this sense, so that the effect may be produced, there is no need for a new divine intervention. In the case of the will, the produced effect is none other than the immanent act of the will. But, can we say that the will, in the act of willing, by a necessary act of willing the universal good, is at the same time in the act of freely willing a definite good? Of course not: it would be saying that it is willing the universal good which determines the desire to access a particular good, which precisely would destroy freedom.
>
> The will, in the act of willing the universal good, therefore remains fundamentally indeterminate with respect to various specific goods, and this is the basis for the freedom of its free act. It may be that the first movement of willing concerning a specific good, when the intelligence does not yet have the necessary discriminations, might simply be a natural and spontaneous willing of a good as such, where the free will cannot intervene; but reason has discovered the limits of the concrete good that is offered to it, and from that moment arises for the will the question of the conscious and deliberate choice: that particular good which at the outset had awakened in him the appetite of pure and simple good, now appears to it with its limitations and imperfections: and in face of such a finite good judged as such, the will is free and undetermined. It may will that good or not will it.
>
> But indeterminacy is not an act, it is a potentiality. The act of the willing of the universal good puts the will in potency to will freely

that particular good or to not will it, or to will another. Who will operate the transition from potentiality to actuality? The will, no doubt, but not without appealing to Him who is the source of all movement, of all transitions from potentiality to actuality; to God, the First Mover. So it must be that our free acts, as free, are caused by God as the source of all activity and movement, so that we can produce them on our level of secondary cause. As well, far from destroying our freedom, it is this divine intervention which, on the contrary, saves it. For, as God, who is First Being and the first source of being communicates to us a participated being constantly supported in existence by His creative action, so also, God, first Love and the source of love, produces in us a participated love where is found, in terms of creation, the great prerogatives of the uncreated Love, that is, the necessary will of the good as such, and the will free of all that are only derived goods. In other words, God, the author of our freedom, is the only one able to move it without breaking the wheels, as it is only a participation in God's own freedom.

And when our willing, by mistake, (...) shall be for an apparent good, that is to say, towards a reality that is not our rational human good, but still a good in a certain respect, without which it could not become an object of appetite for the will, we will need God's help to support our deficient activity and be its mover, certainly not in that which is deficient and deprived of being, but precisely in that which still has being and goodness in spite of it all. For God, who has willed that we should exist as creatures endowed with freedom, owes it to himself that he should ensure in any event the exercise of this freedom, and thus support with His efficiency our free will, even when it turns towards objects that are unworthy of him. In so doing, God does not approve of our sins; neither does he cause an increase of the evil which, as such, is non-being and does not fall, for that reason, under the

Principle of being. But God preserves and supports what makes our dignity and nobility: freedom.[56]

So, can we say that divine providence owes it to itself to attend the intellect and the will of man in pursuit of his personal good and that of the universe. This possibility of direct intervention from God can be entertained by reason with the help of the metaphysics of potentiality and actuality. It can be done by referring to the theory that Maurice de la Taille has developed under the formula of *created actuation by uncreated Act.*[57]

According to this view, God communicates Himself to a human being by uniting Himself directly to it by means for an actuation surpassing created nature. The obediential potentiality is needed for this actuation created by the uncreated Act (i.e. God) and, because of his intellectual soul, it belongs only to man among the corporeal beings. The notion of efficient causality which reflects the natural relationship between the created and the uncreated is not enough to explain how the spiritual soul can be governed by God according to the measure of his intellectual faculties and their freedom. It is therefore useful to have recourse to the notion of direct communication – Communication of Spirit to spirit through a created actuation by the uncreated Act – where God becomes analogically the act of a created potentiality. As the act is communicated to the potentiality to actuate and perfect it, God communicates himself to the potentiality of the human mind and actuates and perfects it as a secondary cause of its own good and of the common good.

It was seen in discussing creation that because of its infinity, divine energy transcends the *formed energy* that has issued from it and

---

[56]Héris Charles V., Op. cit., p. 276-277.

[57]De la Taille, Maurice , "*Actuation created by uncreated act*" Recherche des sciences religieuses, Institut catholique, Paris, 1952, p. 253-268.

therefore cannot be diminished by it in any way. The same is true for the transcendence of the uncreated Act, which may be received in a limiting form by the human potentiality. If we can speak of information, it will only be in the sense given to the information of energy in the theory of Creation which was introduced earlier.[58] In that theory of creation, it was suggested that the idea behind the term *informed energy* or *formed energy* would help connect metaphysics with experimental science. In the theory of the communication of self on the part of God, the term *created actuation* fills the same role. While being distinct from both the *uncreated act* and the *actuated potentiality*, it bridges the gap between these two terms. In the order of nature, the only possible parallel to the distinction between act and actuation is that which distinguishes between the act of existing proper to the spiritual soul and the actuation of the body. The soul gives life to the body, but it is not its actuation, since in death, it remains after the disappearance of that body.

This theory can be applied to social reality, as did P. Delettre. The spirit with which human beings are endowed as a species would remain single if it were not individualized by accidents born of matter. However, the diversity thus produced by matter and assimilated by the divers personal essences[59] retains its unifying principle whereby men tend to form in a social body. This unity of the species, God created it, and he conserves it according to His providential plan. Since the specific difference of man is intelligence, a spiritual faculty, God actuates its unitive potentiality by communicating His own unity to it through love.[60]

---

[58]Some commentators on the theory of "created actuation by uncreated Act" describe it as a "quasi-formal causality."

[59]This is indicated by Boethius in his definition of the person, which is that the person is "an individual substance of a rational nature " (See note 119.)

[60]A question discussed in Part I.

I think this theory is consistent with the position of Thomas Aquinas, who believes that the divine assistance operates[61] ab *intrinseco* and that it adds something to the creature. From the point of view of philosophy, the word assistance means, in this instance, the production of the same effect by the simultaneous action of several causes. The divine assistance thus produces the same effect by the action of the Creator and that by his creature. However, if we exclude a Molinist interpretation of this descriptive definition, we can say that the creature in its operation, as secondary cause, is entirely dependent upon God, the First Cause. If it were in God that we considered this divine assistance we would perceive it as an act of divine providence who desires and foresees the operations of *formed energy*. From this point of view, it would be formally an immanent action and virtually a transitive action. However, the divine assistance takes place not in God but in the creature; so it represents the secondary effect of the divine government according to which the created universe is absolutely dependent on God as to its operation and as to its end.

We have seen that prime matter appears when an energy is informed. Energy and form have their origin in the principle-agent outside of which being is not, neither actually nor virtually. In causal terms, this means that for the conservation of its existence, the corporeal reality requires a formal and efficient material causality, not to mention the causality of finality without which existence would have no meaning. We can therefore consider the divine government as continuous creation: the maintenance of energy information by an absolutely perfect First Cause for a finality that is the ultimate perfection of the same creation. The following comment argues in favor of the

[61]Emile Filion defines the divine assistance as "the absolute dependence of the secondary cause in relation to the first cause in the same operation ." (op. cit., page 156.)

dependence of the body on the principle-agent who can only be incorporeal:

> When the efficient cause, acting through movement, ceases to act, at that moment the becoming of the realities produced ceases as well, and also, when ceases the action of the incorporeal agent, who is the real producer of forms[62], the being of the same realities produced by him likewise will cease. Because it is the form that gives a reality to its being and allows it to exist in its proper specificity. Once a form is actually united to matter[63] the substantial composite that results from this union exists. Says S. Thomas: " *Esse consequitur formam*" Therefore, He who gives form gives being.

> This incorporeal agent, God, (by whom all things are produced, both the corporeal and incorporeal realities), is the author of form and matter. Therefore, the necessary conclusion: if the divine operation were to cease, all things would return immediately to nothingness.[64]

There is a logical distinction between creation and conservation in existence, although they are of a single act in God. Applied to the world of material *formed energy* to which movement belongs as principle, the government is necessarily exercised on a creation already in actuality, though in potentiality of other forms. So, its first effect is the conservation of the marriage between energy and form - in other words, the maintenance of the quantification of energy in the movement of forms. In this context, one can give to movement a

---

[62](*ipse dator formarum* as Thomas would say in *De Potentia*, a. 5 a. 1 sol. 9) Héris , Ch -V "Technical Information", *Le gouvernement divin*, Volume I, Edition du Cerf, Paris, 1958, p. 256.

[63]According to the present theme, matter is already something informed.

[64]*Op. Cit.* #197

notion of direction towards the good which, in the first place, is that of existence. It is not that the material energy subjects the form to movement, but rather that matter is transformable. This notion rejoins the second effect of the divine government and makes it inseparable from the first. Indeed there is only conservation and movement towards the good and true government can only tend towards the good. The principle of this movement is the One who is its source and essence, that is, God. He moves the *formed energies* which he maintains in existence, in order that they, in turn, may move others. Thus, in the movement that comes from God, the *formed energies* move each other towards their common good. This is so in spite of the fact that things become confused for the human mind when it comes to the government of particular goods especially in the case of animate *formed energies* that are irrational (i.e. beasts). It is inevitable that in pursuing its own particular good, the *formed energy* opposes some particular good established in the divine plan. The cat that catches the mouse prevents the mouse's good, which was enshrined in its its nature by the Creator, from reaching its fulfillment. The case of the human person is even more problematic since humans can choose to thwart their own particular good. But in the end, globally, Creation attains its end.

God governs the world by his very presence even within the *formed energy* which He draws to himself. In forming the *energy* from His own virtual energy, it is necessary that God dwells in it immanently in order to maintain its existence because it exist only in participation of his Being. So, by means of the movement of matter and the intelligibility of forms that nature received from Him, God leads the whole universe, down to the inanimate things, to its good. So, it is his presence in the corporeal beings that God draws to himself when he leads them to the unity which is their good, because it is his own image in His creatures that God loves. Aquinas seems to be leaning in that direction when, having said that "God moves as the object of desire and apprehension" he adds that "it does not follow that He always moves as being desired and apprehended by that which he moves; but as being desired and known by himself; for He does all things for His own goodness."[65] Thus, God loves and knows Himself in the things he has created. Reproduced in Nature, these two faculties - love and knowledge - influence each other in their tendency towards their union with God, their ultimate good. This was explained as follows in my book: *The Ontological Foundation of Regency* :

> Here, there is a greater reciprocity of influence, but love unites human beings more effectively than knowledge. However, it is the knowledge of the object's goodness that leads us to love.[66] Without the knowledge that allows us to possess things by internalizing them, union in love is not possible. Indeed, when we desire a material object it is to better apprehend it and possess it through the mind. Also, to enjoy the knowledge of an object can engender love of knowledge itself by stimulating a desire for a greater knowledge. And the source of this desire, like that of any desire that compels us to conquer the good we lack with a view to tasting the joy of resting in its possession, which is love.[67]

> The union resulting from possession, Thomas Aquinas teaches, already exists, inchoately or affectively, in desire. It becomes effective only when it fulfills all the perfection to which the subject was, due to it, in potentiality.[68] In this context, regency is exercised when free will orders its entourage with the acquisition of a common or personal good in mind. However, there would be no tendency towards this good without the desire of love that

---

[65]*Summa Theologica,* I, q. 105, a. 2 .

[66]See *Ibid.,* I- II, q. 27, a. 2

[67]See *Ibid.,* I- II, q. 33 a. 1, ad 2.

[68]See *Ibid.,* I- II, q. 28, a. 1.

yearns for union. As long as the union to the desired good is not actually achieved, love attaches the good to the subject through affection. And when this union with a good being (or considered as good) is successful through love, its act is more comprehensive (though less perfect) than knowledge because, by love, the being which is desired for its goodness is united as it is to the subject, while by means of knowledge, it is united only by an abstract representation which can be assimilated. (The goodness or kindness of the beloved does not need to be fully known, but there must be sufficient apprehension of it to give rise to desire.)

In this context, a question appears, which we notice in passing earlier when we considered the human person as "an individual substance of a rational nature" (as defined by Boethius[69]) : how can God move a free being while respecting his freedom? The free will has for principle a will governed by reason and this principle cannot be violated. So how can God move the human person externally without violating his or her free will? Can someone be moved at the same time by himself and by another? If God moves the person, should He not, by the same token, be accountable for its actions? In *The Ontological Foundation of regency*, these questions where answered in the following way by relying on the philosophy of Thomas Aquinas. It is a matter of the free participation of man in the regency of God's government :

> From the perspective of providence by which God exercises his regency by governing beings who owe Him their existence, human freedom still faces a difficulty, which Thomas Aquinas tries to solve. First, he affirms at the same time the freedom of man and that of God. Knowledge and existence are not in God

---

[69]Boethius, A short treatise on theology: *Opuscula Sacra*, translated, introduced and annotated by Hélène Merle, Les Editions du Cerf, Paris, 1991, p. 59.

what they they are in humans: the Supreme Being has them both at the same time while participated beings acquire them successively. Otherwise, God would be subject to change and imperfection :

"We understand things successively only because we consider each one in themselves, we would have a simultaneous intelligence of them, if they were considered to be in the one and the same being, as we consider the parts in the whole, or as we see various objects in a mirror. God seeing all within himself... sees everything simultaneously and not successively."[70]

Again, the existence out of time is used as an argument by Aquinas to demonstrate that we cannot attribute to God the operations and limitations of the human intellect. However, it remains that man is free, otherwise reason would serve him for nothing. In order to harmonize these two realities, Aquinas distinguishes between the *First Cause* and *secondary causes*. To be free, it suffices for man to be the secondary cause of his actions, while God remains their first cause. The author of the *Summa Theologica* gives, as an analogy of the secondary cause, a man who builds something: he is rightly the cause of what he produces, even if he uses already existing things, of which God is the first cause:

"It is not essential to freedom that a free being be its own cause, as it is not necessary for something to be the cause of another, that it be its first cause. Thus, God is the first cause that moves all natural and voluntary causes. And as by putting natural causes in motion does not mean that their actions are not natural, likewise in acting on voluntary causes does not prevent

---

[70]*Summa*, Q. 14, a.7.

their actions from being voluntary, but rather it gives them this character, because He acts in every being in a manner consistent with what is proper to it."[71]

Free will is at the heart of the idea of regency, since it represents the actions governed by reason. Aquinas considers freedom as an attribute of the will as long as it is rational. The premise of his argument rests on the distinction between the order of specification in which intelligence has primacy, and the order of exercise (or "motor" causes) where primacy belongs to the will. In the order of specification, as we know, the will is necessarily determined by the general welfare or the Absolute Good. In such a case, the freedom of choice disappears, but there is still a certain freedom of spontaneity since the option for this determining good is done by oneself without being pushed by another. We have seen, moreover, that God can move the will without infringing on freedom. If it is naturally driven by the sovereign good, man has the freedom to choose the means to achieve it.[72]

Violence is done to the will only when there is external influence contrary to its inclination. However, the inclination of the free will to its good comes from God and therefore it cannot be otherwise. It is the same for predetermined corporeal being: the inclination of the plant to grow upward comes from its God-given nature and it cannot be otherwise. Man moves freely under an intrinsic principle, but this principle depends on an extrinsic principle: God, the first principle.

Man therefore moves freely toward the good he perceives by virtue of the potentiality that God gives him. The good is perceived by the

---

[71] *Opus cit.*, Q. 8, a.1

[72] Chabot, Jean-Nil, *The Ontological Foundation of Regency*, p.8-9

intellect, but the latter can only adhere to the object presented to it with certainty and evidence. In other words, intelligence adheres to its object by grasping its reason for being. Indeed, Being – the universal essence of all that is - has in itself every reason to be and provides to the intelligence its proper object. God is the universal Being, the intellectual corporeal beings move their intelligence only in as much as they participate in Him. Ultimately, it is God who moves their intelligence, directly or through intermediaries.

What has been just been said of intelligence also applies to the will since its proper object is also that which is most universal, that is to say, Being, God's essence. Nothing can attract the will other than what has the aspect of good and the universal Good possesses in itself all the goods. This is why the intellectual corporeal beings have the good for right reason only in as much as they are participating of God, the supreme good. So, it is always God who moves the intellect and will. If man can make mistakes, it is always under the aspect of good, but while aiming at a particular good without recognizing its relative value in relation to the universal good . Thomas Aquinas says it well when he writes that "all actions are produced for a good, real or apparent, and nothing on the other hand is good or appears to be so, without possessing some similarity by participation to the sovereign Good, which is God"[73]. Although he is naturally driven by the sovereign Good, man has the freedom to choose the means to achieve it.

Thus, in the case of the free corporeal being God moves the will by providing the appropriate object and by causing its ability to choose. Although He is the first Cause of the voluntary act, God does not prevent the will to move itself as secondary cause, since He maintains its freedom by giving it its own inclination.

---

[73] *Summa Theologica*, I, q. 105, a.5.

Reason, in the choices obligated by its will, can affirm that man is not left to himself. This can be demonstrated from the principle that a thing cannot cause what it does not have in itself. So, what the human personality possesses through its participation in divinity (life, intellect, will) God possesses in himself perfectly and infinitely. However, the human will is moved by the love of the form he perceives as the end of his art, and he strives to reach it. Since "the moving agent cannot move a mobile in a sufficient manner unless its virtue exceeds or, at least, equals the passive virtue of the mobile", as Thomas Aquinas said, "even more so, since God is the source of human faculties, does he love his creation and want to lead it effectively to its final end."[74]

God works through secondary causes, according to the order of their perfection, as in the following text regarding regency :

> Ultimately, it is to *being* (that is perfection and last actuation) that we must go, in order to find the principle of regency, because the unity on which it rests depends on its degree of actuation and perfection. Everything finds its deepest internal unity in its being as where it is subsistent and distinct. God is the Being of beings which is why everything tends towards unity in him. It is also by being that everything belongs to the universe as it is the whole of all what is in God. No creature can be outside of that *whole* which is the universe. As Aristotle, indeed, wrote: "Being is that which all beings have in common."[75] Later, he repeats the same statement in another way: "Being in essence receives as many meanings as there are categories, since the meanings of being are as numerous as the categories."[76] Which is the case,

---

[74]*Ibid.*, A. 4.
[75]*Metaphysics*, IV, 3, 1005 a, 23-33.
[76]*Ibid.*, V. 7, 1017 a 25 .

primarily, for the category of substance because it encompasses all the others. So, it is that we find in the whole of creatures a universal relationship which they take as much from their common origin and their essential dependence on their first principle as from their return converging towards it. In the universe described by Thomas Aquinas, everything holds together and everything is in accord. The superior beings exercise their regency by communicating their superior riches to their inferior for the common good of the universe. This all relates to God, the supreme King, to whom the hierarchy of forms is subjected. However, each being considered as an individual thing, escapes the totalitarianism of the created whole because everything exists by God and for Him before existing for others. Aquinas insists that the order that connects creatures to God is prior to that which connects them to each other.

We can define a thing in terms of its relations with the world around it. But this definition cannot tell the whole being of this particular thing, because the value it has comes first since it is subsistent. In its subsistence, the thing refers itself directly to God and can not be reduced to its relations with the created universe. Thus the ontological order of regency is exercised primarily on the divine plane, from God to his creatures, and then only on the level of finite beings from the higher beings to inferior beings. If the principal marks of regency are unity and power, their perfect manifestation would be the actualization of forms by means of the communication of being. God alone has the ultimate degree regency.[77]

Because of his intelligence and free will, man is at the top of reality and that is why the regency of the world falls to him, first. We have

---

[77]Chabot, Jean-Nil, op. cit., p. 11.

seen that as a secondary cause, this regency is effective only under the First Cause to which it is submitted. But since man exercises his causality through intelligence and will, which are spiritual faculties, it is through them that the effectiveness of the First Cause is communicated. Among the corporeal beings moving towards their finitude (their second entelechy), man is the only one with a spiritual soul that can respond freely to God's initiative. In the work cited above, this idea is developed by reference to Aristotle`s treatise *De Anima*.This concerns the first act (or first entelechy) representing that which the human person has received from nature and the second act (second entelechy) representing that which was acquired by the individual and added to his nature.[78]

The first entelechy is mainly the work of creation, but it also belongs to the work of conservation which ensues as the logical consequence of the creative act. In the case of the human person, the second entelechy applies in particular to the government of self.[79] However, as we have said, man, while being free, does not does not escape divine government.

---

[78]The first entelechy means "the act done as opposed to the act being done, and perfection resulting from this achievement" and then "the form or reason that determines the actualization of a potentiality" (Lalande André, *Vocabulaire technique et critique de la philosophie,* Presses universitaire de France, Paris, 1956.) critical vocabulary of philosophy, University Presses of France, Paris, 1956.) A term coined by Aristotle, eg: "Of the dynamism of the limited natural physical agent to a motion according to a single local direction"- ad unum – beginning with "the movement of plants occurring according to local opposite directions" (from *De Anima*, II, 2, 413 a 25-3) - Ad ambo - and the "hand capable of taking everything and of seizing everything "- ad omnia – up to the" human soul which is, in a certain way, whole existing "(from De Anima, III, 8, 431 b 21-22 and 432 a 1-3) - *ad infinita.*

[79]Evil, as long as it is a refusal to participate in Being, belongs to this second entelechy. The divine act, that of the first entelechy, can only be perfect and good.

We saw, also, that matter has its origin in the spirit and that it is in potentiality of the spirit. It passes from the inertia of dead (or purely material) substances to plant life; from plant life to sentient life; from sentient life to rational life. In the psyche of the rational life, there is an aspiration, as a seed of immortality, which indicates a final return to the spirit. This psychological character exists and seems to have always existed in all peoples. It is part of human nature and only an intellectual formation (or deformation) can succeed to remove it, if not entirely, at least in its intellectual conscience. This intuition, which is also that of the infinite, expresses itself in different ways in different cultures. In the Judeo-Christian culture, if understood according to St. Paul, *it is not the spiritual that first appears, rather it is the natural and then the spiritual. It is sown a natural body; it is raised a spiritual body.*[80] However, that matter be in potentiality to the spirit requires an efficient cause, external, but acting immanently in this case in order to move it to actuality .

---

[80]Cor. 15: 46 and 15:44

PART IV

Human government by means of laws

The idea of a free return of the rational creature to its principle having been introduced, this next section will discuss how man orders the exercise of his free will while remaining true to his nature and obeying the attraction of his own destiny. This is the goal that man must freely undertake in order to succeed in his vocation as secondary cause in the return of corporeal beings to their First Principle. Since this teleological undertaking is voluntary and therefore proper to the human person, it concerns morality, More specifically, it relates to the virtues, because these well ordered habits help man's sense of duty regarding the fulfillment of his ultimate end. "The great motive of man's activity is a sense of duty which controls the exercise of his freedom."[81] But, it will be primarily a matter of the law, because the latter has the specific function of a principle for the virtues and for morality in general. Having the function of a principle, human law (or positive law) is nevertheless inspired by divine government and so is eternal law and natural law.

The distinction between the divine government and the eternal law was established at the beginning of the previous earlier. For his part Thomas Aquinas offers the following precision:

> It was seen that the law is nothing else but a dictate of practical reason emanating from the leader who governs a perfect community. Now, it is evident, granted that the world is governed by Divine Providence, that the whole community of the universe is governed by Divine Reason. Wherefore, the very Idea of the government of things in God as the Supreme Ruler of the

[81]Pope Paul VI, *A Nazareth,* From an address given at the Basilica of the Asnnunciation, at Nazareth, January 5, 1964.

universe, has the nature of a law. And since the Divine Reason's conception of things is not subject to time but is eternal (...) therefore it is that this kind of law must be called eternal.[82]

This eternal law, therefore, consists of the general principles by which God governs his creation with justice. Justice is manifested in acts which are designed to give everyone his rights, that is to say the things to which he is necessarily entitled[83] in order to achieve his own good and fulfill his responsibilities to the common good. Since Creation is not an absolute necessity for God, nothing is due to it on His part - which makes us wonder what constitutes the justice of God. However, because of the perfection of the Creator, we admit that there is in him a certain relative necessity. The *formed energies,* or so-called "creatures", and the whole they form, evolve according to the universal order inscribed in them by their author. The order in which a place and a proper operation are assigned to each of these *formed energies* and to all of them as a whole reflects the guidelines from the creative act of God. The latter, in his perfection and infinite power, does not disorder the laws he has established in his work, but, on the contrary, he respects them so well that experimental science can rely on them even when ignoring their transcendental origin .

Since all authentic human laws cannot evade the order of relationships and imperatives established within and between the corporeal beings by the Eternal Law, it is important to know whether it falls under the divine will or under the divine intelligence. Since Creation is accomplished freely, it can be attributed to the will.

---

[82] Summa Theologica, I- II, q. 91 a. 1.

[83]. Someone or a group may necessarily be entitled to something. Thus the average person is entitled to the law in order to fulfill its destiny. This destiny falls within the common good and depends on it. The State is the guarantor of the common good and therefore of human rights. So, the social body responsible for the law, that is the State, has the duty to ensure human rights.

However, a previous part of this book showed that in the evolutionary work of Creation there is an intelligence that operates towards of an end. If there is finality, there must also be intelligence and ideas; if there is operation, there are also energy and will. What else can we conclude other than Creation is being freely accomplished and that it must be, by the same token, also a work of the will? But if we ascribe an arbitrary decree of the divine will as principle of the universal order would it not deny wisdom the part that belongs to it in the finality of things? To conclude clearly, it is worth having recourse to the fundamental theses of the Thomistic doctrine.

To begin, those Thomistic theses are based on the principle, which was demonstrated earlier, that God is pure Act and that He is absolutely simple. Everything about him is eternal and infinite. His knowledge of Himself embraces all existence, as well as His own perfection and His love of it, and all this is but one and the same infinite act. As Supreme Being, He understands everything that exists in reality and everything that exists virtually. Therefore, it is only analogically that we can conceive that the effects of divine power originated either from the intelligence or the will.

We see an image of the divine perfection when we consider man as a microcosm. Indeed, the human soul, unique and indivisible principle of human life, allows this analogy. Because it is spiritual, the human soul not only distributes life and its function to each part of the body but it is also the principle of acts properly intellectual. Its influence is exerted on the level of thought as well as on the nutritive and reproductive level. There is therefore in this microcosm a hierarchy of function and perfection, as can be deduced from what seen previously. To the vegetative perfection, it provides proper specific functions, then comes the sensory perfection of the beast and, finally at the highest level, the intellectual perfection crowns it all. This is how we compare the various potentialities that we observe as effects of the human soul to those we distinguish in God .

When considering Creation we can assign the divine attributes to one or the other of its effects. Thus, when God brings essences to existence by introducing limiting forms (or proportions) in His infinite energy, we can say that He acts under the aspect of his free will. On the other hand, in the formation of corporeal beings resulting from this creative act and in the ordination of their mutual relations, it is rather the aspect of His sovereign wisdom that must be recognized .

Because God is absolutely simple we must infer that in Him ideas (or forms in the context of Creation) are not distinct. While man results from a marriage of act and potentiality in which thought can only be accidental (always moving and able to change), in God (in whom there is no potentiality) thought is one and eternal, without any possibility of acquisition or change. Although the movement of thinking is contrary to the divine nature, we nevertheless speak of ideas that are in God. So, there is a need for an explanation and we cannot offer it in a better way than by quoting Thomas Aquinas:

> Inasmuch as God knows His own essence perfectly, He knows it according to every mode in which it can be known. Now it can be known not only as it is in itself, but as it can be participated into by creatures according to some degree of likeness. But every creature has its own proper species, according to which it participates in some degree of likeness to the divine essence. Therefore, so far as God knows His essence as capable of such imitation by any creature, He knows it as the particular type and idea of that creature: and in like manner as regards other creatures. So it is clear that God understands the many particular types of things, and these are many Ideas.[84]

Sertillanges comments that "it would certainly hinder the fact that God knows many things, if this were about independent objects that fall by themselves directly under knowledge. It was said earlier that God cannot actually think but one thing, which is Himself. But in Himself, He can conceive eveything in dependence of His essence which, in His perfect unity, represent everything to Him."[85]

Since God is the infinite Being outside of whom nothing exists, because everything owes Him its own existence, nothing can completely emulate Him and that is why corporeal beings are necessarily created in numbers. The possible worlds, are the various manners of resemblance that are susceptible of participation in the divine essence. A remote comparison would be that of the architect who would have produced several plans for a house to be built. There will be several factors that will influence his choice - such as the wishes of customers, availability of materials, etc. - but, ultimately, it will depend on his free will. Once built, the house will fulfill its role without the architect having to intervene. The divine architect applies His volition and His intellection similarly when, among all the worlds that are possible to him, he chooses to create one of them. Also the creative action of God that we attribute to his will is just as much a work of wisdom. Thomas Aquinas stated it as follows :

> In God, intellect and will do not really differ, so that the fact that the will receives a direction from thought and is determined by it to something, it is not determined to something else; it moves according to its nature, because it is natural for it to act according to its wisdom.[86]

---

[84]*Somme théologique*, I, q.15, a. 2.

[85] Dieu, *Explanatory Notes*, p. 362, Dresclée & Cie, Paris, 1963.

[86]Thomas Aquinas, De Veritate, q. 23, s. 6 .

Because our imperfect thought must operate according to the spatial and temporal divisions, it is not possible for us to understand the divine simplicity. We must be content to consider various aspects of it. It is therefore natural for us to affirm the compliance of the voluntary action of God to the order of his wisdom. This wisdom has constituted the corporeal beings from type-models (that is to say, the ideas) and potentiality (that is to say, energy). Since they govern energy, ideas form the immanent law of natural things according to Creative Wisdom's plan for the universe, which is a reflection of His eternal law. Therefore:

> The will does not have the character of primitive rule, it has normative value only insofar as it is itself regulated by reason and intelligence, not only in ourselves, but in God. And so, that on which the value of justice depends above all, is the wisdom of the divine intelligence which constitutes all things in the required proportions and within themselves in relation to their causes. It is on this proportion that the value of created justice is constituted. To say that justice depends on the will only is to say that God's will does not act with wisdom...[87]

On the other hand, when applied to morality, legal justice has effect only on what is contingent et subjected to free will. Since nature is identified with law, predetermined corporeal beings obey their natural determinations and are not subject to morality. In fact, what falls under human government, is only what man can do himself. Everything that belongs essentially to the order of nature escapes man's government because, in this, one finds a law higher than the human law which governs man. Analogously, we can say of human law that it consists of rules derived from the established order of nature, just as the Eternal law (taken from our human point of view)

---

[87]Ibid.

consists of rules derived from the order established by the divine government. So, nature is not subject to human law, but rather it merges with it. A human law that is repugnant to being merged with nature does not require obedience, because there cannot be any contradiction between nature and law. Thomas Aquinas affirms it:

> Natural law is a participation of the eternal law. That is why it remains without any change: it takes this character of immobility and perfection from the divine reason which constituted nature while human reason, on the contrary, is changing and imperfect. Moreover, natural law contains only a few general precepts, which remain the same; on the contrary, the law established by man contains particular precepts, according to the various cases that arise.[88]

And then:
> A measure should be fixed as much as possible. In changing things, there cannot be something absolutely immutable. This is why human law cannot be fully immutable.[89]

Good conduct and morality also involve virtues. They operate in the midst of different principles of action, some favorable to good, the others favorable to evil. Committed among these influences man cannot act alone. The intellect and the will of his fellowmen come to his aid when he associates with them to form autarchies increasingly able to provide him with peace and a life that is truly human. Thus, a State appears, whose prudent laws allow man to hope for a peaceful life in an honest and comfortable standard of living. But above all, God is there as the principle immanent in all things, but especially in all spiritual corporeal beings, acting as their first Cause in all their

---

[88] Ibid.
[89] Ibid.

operations as we have seen. The theory of Maurice de la Taille has demonstrated that a personal God can act as principle of the volitional power of man when this one applies himself to satisfy his appetite for good. This divine action is immediately in the soul, virtuous men apply it to the observance of the law established by God as a beacon to show human beings the paths that lead to their ultimate end. Man has his hand in determining these beacons, as he is the participating image of the divine activity. This human participation in the divine order will be the positive law, which Thomas Aquinas defined as "an order of reason for the common good, established and promulgated by the one who has the care of the community"[90]. Looking at this positive law from the perspective of the four causes that constitute the being of all things, we find that the order of reason acts as *formal cause* (intrinsic); the common good as *final cause*; the one who has care of the community and establishes and promulgates as *efficient cause*; and finally, as *material cause*, the community (or human actions within the community). Since positive law identifies itself to the government (being its form) we can attribute to the latter the same relation as to the four causes. Charles Journet does so by means of the definition of Thomas Aquinas : "The king is the person - *efficient cause* - governing - *formal cause* - the multitude of a city - *material cause* - for the common good - *final cause*."[91]

Aquinas begins his treatise on laws with a general exposition that elaborates on their foundation, that is to say, on a deliberate human act and its effect. He does this, first, by stating that the power to act is put into operation by the will which depends, in turn, on the judgment made by reason. It shows itself as a value judgment in favor of a particular end and its proper means, since, in order to found and guide the operation from the beginning, general and universal

---

[90]Ibid. q. 97, a.1, ad 1 and 2.

[91]Charles Journet , in his preface to the book *The Kingdom*, trans. Claude Roquet, Librairie du Dauphin, Paris , 1931 , p. XIX.

principles, which reason abstracts from natural law, are necessary. Intelligence does the same in the speculative sciences, when it applies its research to the stable phenomena where human action is not a determinant. So, intelligence simply interpret these phenomena in the light of axioms which serve as principles, such as that of *identity* or that of *contradiction*. Then as it becomes *practical* for the actions to be executed, reason acts in the same way, since it always operates in accordance with the order of reality. It has recourse, in the same way, to the enlightening of universal principles so as to guide the search for the true good and discover the appropriate means to attain it. These indicating principles of human actions are the laws. Thomas Aquinas affirms this as follows:

> In our actions that manifest themselves externally, it is necessary to distinguish the operation itself and the work carried out, for example the action of building and the building itself; similarly, in the intellectual operations, it is necessary to distinguish the action of reason itself, which is nothing other than thinking and reasoning, and secondly what is the result produced by this activity. In the speculative order, this result is called the definition, then the proposition and finally the syllogism and the demonstration. But practical reason also uses reasoning to judge the things are to be done. (...) So it is normal to find in practical reason, something that plays in relation to the operations to be executed, that is, the role that the principle fulfills in relation to the conclusions in the speculative reason. Precisely those universal propositions of practical reason ordained to actions are nothing other than what we call laws.[92]

These laws are created diversely and their degree of causality depends, as we shall see, on their proximity to the first Principle or

---

[92]Thomas Aquinas, *Summa Theologica* , I- II, q. 90, a. 1.

First Cause. Those that are deduced from our social and reasoning human nature require for their validity that they have an immediate convenance with that nature. It suffices, for those that are established by authority and custom, that they have an indirect convenance with human nature or that they are not in contradiction with it[93]. This second category of laws concerns the necessary or contingent norms imposed on the human free will for the purpose of determining its obligations and its rights. Obligations determine the actions to be performed for the common good and the rights determine the justice of the attribution of the common good to the individual.

Since we are in the Thomistic tradition, we establish with the author of the *Treatise on Law*, (<u>Summa Theoligica</u>, Question 90) a distinction between the judgment of conscience and the judgment of free will: the former operates in the domain of theory, while the latter finds its application in the practical domain.[94] Free will has for object the choice *decided upon* rather than what *should be done*, which is why it refers mostly to the will. The correctness of the action depends on the correctness of the judgment that initiated the choice since it is its effect. The perspectives, that can be taken to determine that judgment, are many and complex - correctness depends on the choices that are made in each particular case. While acknowledging that the Absolute Good necessarily determines the desire of the will, it must be recognized that the specific choices required by this Good involve difficulties. Indeed, the final decision follows the choice resulting from the deliberations that were offered to the different opportunities. This choice is primarily a matter of reason, which determines - based on laws – the necessary moral value that will allow the will to act with rectitude. For instance, reason may abdicate

---

[93]For instance, the traffic law stating that one is to drive of the right (or left) side of the road has an indirect convenance with human nature (human life should be protected) and the contrary specification (left or right) is not in contradiction with it.

[94]Thomas Aquinas, *De Veritate* , q . 23 , s. 6.

its responsibility by leaving the disorderly passions or perversity to integrate themselves into the laws that man establishes in full freedom, so that these oppose to the immutable law inscribed in nature. It is reasonable to believe that in such an instance, He who established the principle of all laws comes to the help of legislators and of those who are the subjects of the legal imperatives. The *created actuation by an uncreated act* provides a way by which a human being, assisted by the law and moved inwardly by God's action, can respond to the appeal of the good.

At the beginning of this discourse, God was seen as the First Principle of the Law which leads to the conclusion that only a legislation derived from divine law can bind the human conscience. For, does not law itself, being the imperative rule of action for reasonable and free corporeal beings, have its principle from the very Author of reason and the universal order? Whether he wants it or not, man is ordained to the universe to which he belongs and therefore must agree with the laws that are inscribed therein by his Creator, even before considering the constraints imposed by society. Everything stems from the fact that the order of the universe is attributable to God, as was previously demonstrated. Having established the existence of a First Cause, we can judge that it also incorporates within the order of the universe, all the corporeal beings which necessarily depend on it for their existence and their becoming.

So, how to interpret the definition of the law as it has been stated? Aquinas says, first, that it is something of reason. It is for the intellect a question of examining the existential reality according the order of reason, in order to empower the will to find the proper ways to carry out the specific end it intends. The argument is that the command belongs to reason, since it causes the execution of the means towards of their ends. Such an order requires reason.

The law has, for primary function, to help man in regulating his life by directing his actions to his ultimate end. It is a function applied to an ethic, which is none other than compliance with the order of the universe. We have seen that the human mind has the ability not only to understand the formal structures embedded in things, but that it also has the power to bring judgment on the objects of his reason so as to reform and restructure them into new orders that will enrich man's social and physical environment. When the new order to achieve will focus on the reality outside the will for which intelligence must respect the determinations, it will then apply to the arts: either the rational art or logic art, whereby reason ordains itself for the attainment of the truth, or the liberal arts, in the exercise of their acquired and cultivated faculties, or even the mechanical arts, when it reorganizes the material causalities according to an instrumental order so as to be served by them. On the other hand, it will be an ethical issue when human reason strives to establish an order that addresses the acts of the will itself. This question pertains to the law because "the rule and measure of human acts is reason," says Thomas Aquinas, and he goes on to say that "reason alone directs to an end, and the end is the first principle of the voluntary act.[95]

From its objective point of view, the law considered in its relation to justice brings additional light to its regulatory and ordering role in the voluntary activity of man. Indeed, it is by considering it according the whole of the human activities it regulates, rather than within the confines of human conscience, that the law reveals the harmony which exists in the order of the universe. The political order reflects the same harmony that exists in the things of natural world. When we examine the law in relation to justice, we do so as an objective content, because it is the requirements of order and of being which then comes into play. As to legislation, it is a mandatory order that the

---

[95]*Summa Theologica* , I- II, q. 90, a.1

author introduces in human activity as a condition for happiness, but which already exists in the connections that nature imposed immediately on the pre-determined corporeal beings and imposes mediately on the free corporeal beings. The law precludes the random effects that would occur without any causes and make it impossible to know the reality which depends on the order of reason. Therefore, there is in society and in nature a need for organization coming from agents who are themselves coordinated in a whole.

The regulatory function exercised by the law as it determines and dictates the relationship between rational corporeal beings adds even more precisions to what distinguishes it from justice. The latter signifies, first of all, that which belongs to each part of the whole. It encompasses two concepts: firstly, what is due - a notion containing a certain necessity; then the idea of fairness and proportion between the reality of the whole and that of the the part. What we can say of this proportion which exists between things of the same kind, we can also say of equality. The proportion of equality is useful to justice when seeking to enforce respect for the law by rendering to everyone his due. Objectively, we can say that justice is the thing rightly proportionate - that is to say the just and right thing. Abstractly it applies to the idea of proportion itself .

The order imposed by the law on corporeal beings presupposes the existence of specific relations. These relations are pre-determined in the case of irrational corporeal beings and so it is not necessary for the latter to be aware of them. This because the actions of each species reflect proportionally the particularities of its nature. If the agent is a beast, it will act proportionally to the particularities of its nature or according to his instinctive judgment, that is to say, without abstracting the idea that is the principle of its action. Man, on the contrary, abstracts from his relationship with reality the order that determines the suitability of his actions so as to create from it his notion of law. Because it stems from reason, this notion lies beyond the immediate human necessity and is realized on the basis on free will. What is due to it and what it owes to others is brought to the judgment of its practical reason in order to determine from it the proper rule. Finally, since the rational being possesses the moral faculty to serve or not to serve the common good determined by the law, the latter can only be attributed to the responsible person who recognizes its correlation with duty. The existence of the law depends, in fact, on the respect that men pay to their duty towards it. The justice of reasonable agents has for measure the compliance of their actions with the law.

To complete what has been said about the distinction between justice and law, it is opportune to look at Thomas Aquinas' comment on the subject:

> Just as there pre-exists in the mind of the craftsman an expression of the things to be made externally by his craft, which expression is called the rule of his craft, so too there pre-exists in the mind an expression of the particular just work which reason determines, and which is a kind of rule of prudence. If this rule is expressed in writing it is called a "law", which according to Isidore (*Etym.* v, 1) is "a written decree": and so law is not the same as justice, but an expression of justice.[96]

As an idea informs energy and acts as Primary Cause of the corporeal being, so does reason rule the will and acts as the main cause of not only the wording of the law but also of its imposition. While intelligence has for its first real object the apprehended reality, that is to say, the truth, the good to be actualized also has the truth for principle, since intelligence exercises its power in two ways, either by

---

[96] Ibid., *II- II* , *q . 57, a. 1*

means of the speculative intellect or by means of the practical intellect. Aquinas gives the following explanation:

> The one includes the other, because what is true is a certain good, otherwise it would not be desirable; and what is good is a certain truth, otherwise it would not be intelligible. Therefore, since the object of desire can be the truth, as it represents a good, likewise the object of the practical intellect is the operable good, considered under the reason of truth. Both intellects know the truth; but here, it is action-oriented truth.[97]

According to the order of reason, truths are deduced from certain principles although it is not without connecting to reality through experience. While the direction of these deductions depends on principles, particularly in the order of speculation – as we may consider, for example, the axioms of identity, of contradiction, of causality, etc. - in the order of the practical, reason provides the will with the principle of its action by making the latter intelligible. Thus, when the will seeks the good of its object, the judgments that guide its action come from the principles of reason and the decisions result from this process.

When a subject makes a decision for a goal, he does it by deliberating on the practical means to take. Having chosen the method that suits the circumstances of the particular application he says to himself: "So, that's what I should do." Practical reason will have proceeded according to the order of truth if the choice meets the requirement for its authenticity, that is to say, the accomplishment of a human good. The role of the law in this development is to provide the necessary principles for the judgments and the reasonings, which in turn will provide the means with their function as intermediary ends

---

[97]Ibid.

with a view to attain the ultimate end. The law is also the standard which indicates to us our rights and duties; it measures our actions so as to make their moral value known to us.

The effect of the law is therefore to determine the judgment of the moral conscience and to bring it to a decision, that is to say, the practical judgment. This relates to free will - it no longer determines what should be done, but what applies to the will. If this applies the judgment of conscience to the intelligence which it moves, then we say that it is just and right. But because of bad habits or unruly passions, the will can be perverted by letting itself be mesmerized by the anticipation of some pleasure or be carried away by lust. For order to rule in human action, it is necessary, therefore, that the free will be directed towards real goodness rather than be conquered by the influences of the moment. The law then provides assistance, because its role is to order human action, while being subject to the discretion of its author. It shows the will the direction to follow in order to achieve the ultimate goal, the purpose of any regulation . "The law denotes a principle directing actions to their end,"[98] says Thomas Aquinas.

Among the specific forms comprised in the law that directs human action to its ultimate end, there are some that have a necessity by right. These are the ones that come from human nature and are essentially concordant to it. The others, those from the laws already in force, have a actual necessity. Because the destiny of each one cannot be realized perfectly outside of the social body, achieving the ultimate goal of each part requires its participation to the common good without which there cannot be a particular good. This participation must necessarily be determined by none other than the legitimate authority .

---

[98]Ibid., I- II, q. 93 a.3.

As a result of what has been accepted, it is necessary that the rational and social being acts according to his nature and contributes to his happiness as well as that of his entourage in obedience to the legitimate laws of his country or his nation. The order established by law constitutes justice: the necessity that laws be obeyed therefore applies by extension to the juridical order that governs all relations with one's neighbours and with society in general. Since our perspective is that of philosophy, which knows things by their causes, we consider the legal order in its ultimate end, that is, the supreme good. The juridical order is therefore incorporated in that of morality, because we consider it to be consistent with the obligations of conscience which include the duties and rights of the people who make up society. Indeed, the individual must sacrifice himself to the social order just as the part must sacrifice itself to the whole. This question was developed in Le fondement ontologique de la royauté, according to the following text:

> Thomas Aquinas in defining the relationship of the part to the whole, explains that the perfection of the part does not reside in the singular being without reference to the entirety to which it belongs, but that it fulfills itself only in function of the whole.[99] Thus, the part tends towards the whole which conditions it for a certain good, a perfection or a superior being. Indeed, as part of the whole, what it is comes from this entirety to which it belongs[100] and identifies with it.[101] Identity, however, is not a value, because the whole is greater than the part which depends on it. What is the same, is the perfection which is proper to them, but it is greater in the whole because it contributes, in different forms, to the perfection of the other parts; imperfect identity, also, because

---

[99]Cf. ibid., I, q.61, a.3 .

[100] Cf. Ibid. II-II, q.58, a.5

[101] Ibid. II-II, q.61, a.1

the part is limited in its ability to participate in the perfection of the whole. Thus the regency of creatures is limited to their ability to participate in the kingdom of God who is the transcendent whole of all created beings.

"Not only does the part find its identity and perfection (without, however, being equal to it) in the whole, but it can also find its efficiency and capacity when acting in union with the whole. There is identity in the action also, since the part acts according to the whole. But here again, the identity is imperfect, because the action of the whole is greater in its parts than they are by themselves.[102] The action is a manifestation of an immanent part of the agent. Among the beasts, it reflects the instinct; in the creature endowed with reason and will, it reflects the personality. Therefore, the action is what it is according to the life of the agent which is its whole. Similarly, the action of a part or of a member of the agent depends on the active life of the living being. So, it is by giving oneself to the living whole and by loving the common good in it more than one's own good that the members enjoy the good life."

In addition, this whole, which is society, can generate demanding duties, even sacrifice, only if it is, itself, an authority endowed with rights. Now, it has no authority but that which comes from the moral law. "When all or a great many agree", affirms Thomas Aquinas, "they cannot be entirely in error."[103] Universality or absolute majority is certainly a good indication for legislators, because then they can assume the normality of a bill, especially if the social life manifest its constant agreement at any time and in any place. However, experience shows that general errors are possible. In such cases, the law schools are required to return to morality and judge social

---

[102] Cf. ibid., I, q. 75, s. 2

[103] Thomas Aquinas, 7, *Ethics,*

institutions according to the common good and the stable norms of justice.[104] When sketching the outline of justice and the foundation of the law in general, Aquinas follows the guidelines of Aristotle by founding them on the order of nature. This foundation is the order such as it is inscribed in the very nature of man by the creative will. Thus, by attributing the unshakable foundation of the natural order to the divine wisdom, man can give to the moral obligation its effectiveness. It is no more a question of the duty imposed by a sovereign authority but the necessity of participation in Being, because when human justice participates in natural law it participates in the divine law.

The law is the work of practical reason when it serves as a guide to the will in the ordering of the means used to achieve a goal that reflects the general good. The execution refers to the will and depends on reason without which there cannot be a relation of cause to effect.

Thomas Aquinas, referring to all laws, says they come from both reason and the will of the legislator. If it pertains to the natural and divine law, the provenance is of the "reasonable will of God" and in the case of human law the provenance is of "the will of man, regulated by reason." Reason acts by providing the formal cause which regulates the action of the will. The will acts by providing the efficient cause which moves reason to its proper act as a formal cause. Such an exchange between reason and will produce two kinds of causalities of which one is practical reason and other speculative reason. All this is consistent with the deep analysis of human acts that the philosophy of Thomas Aquinas opposes to the affirmative which argues that the law comes first from the will.

---

[104] L.13 Such an obligation is presented to us today concerning the right to life.

As for the Count de Vareilles, he argues that the legislature's intention to assert the right of judgment is an important element of the law. He writes:

> The second essential element of the compulsory rule is the will of the legislator to force his subjects to follow the judgment of reason. Without this commitment, the judgment of reason transmitted by the authority to its subjects would be a mere advice or lesson. This element is the only one which is exclusively proper to commandment; it is therefore its constitutive element par excellence.[105]

Suarez and others have taught that the effectual edict, *ordinatio*, discussed by Thomas Aquinas means an order of the will, considered as a rule, whose origin is from reason. It is doubtful, however, that in speaking of the ordering of reason, Aquinas is implying an order of the will. It is true that, according to the teaching of the Summa Theologica, the law brings the *imperium* of the leader externally for diffusion. However, he shows that the voluntary act of the command represents an act of reason whose power of movement comes beforehand from the will. This is what he says in analyzing the voluntary act as follows:

> Now, command is essentially indeed an act of the reason: for the commander orders the one commanded to do something, by way of intimation or declaration; and to order thus by intimating or declaring is an act of the reason. Now the reason can intimate or declare something in two ways. First, absolutely: and this intimation is expressed by a verb in the indicative mood, as when one person says to another: "This is what you should do." Sometimes, however, the reason intimates something to a man

---

[105] Vareilles , conte de, *Les principes fundamentaux du droit,* Pichon , Paris, 1889 , p.14, n.11. Trans. J.N.C.

by moving him thereto; and this intimation is expressed by a verb in the imperative mood; as when it is said to someone: "Do this." Now the first mover, among the powers of the soul, is the will, as stated above (Q. 9, A. 1). And since, therefore, the second mover does not move save by virtue of the first mover, it follows that the very fact that the reason moves by commanding, is due to the power of the will. Consequently, it follows that command is an act of reason which presupposes an act of the will, in virtue of which reason, by its command, moves (the power) to the execution of the act.[106]

The idea of obligation seems to lead some to believe that the order is solely from the will, because they suppose it follows a simple formulation and makes it compelling. They agree that reason enlightens the will and guides it to justice, but that the law owes its power to the will alone. Without it, it is believed, there is only a statement of principle; so, it is "the constitutive element par excellence" of the law. The argument follows that if it were not so, how could we justify that a leader, even legitimate, can impose on others the necessity to act according to his will? Since there is a hierarchy of Being, can we not, also, say that there is a parallel hierarchy of wills? The Supreme Being would impose himself initially as the first principle and his subordinates would participate in his authority. Jean-Jacques Rousseau attempted to escape this first source of authority without setting aside voluntarism and in order to do so, he had to invent the *social contract* because it was necessary to have an authoritarian principle which would impose the order of society by restricting individual freedoms. The agreement to which everyone subscribes voluntarily by giving up some of their autonomy so as to make life in society possible and that constitutes, in his opinion, the source of authority.

---

[106] *Summa Theologica* , I- II, q. 17 a. 1.

The law which takes its value solely from the will of the leader who invents it, without having recourse to the foundation of the first principles determined by reason, undermines the freedom of his subjects. According Leon Duguit, who calls it *subjective justice*, this justice has no *raison d'être* and must be replaced with *objective justice*. The latter would result from an abstract conception, but from a conception emanating from the solidarity that is characteristic of the nation. The State which would implement such a justice would find its subject complying with the law by virtue of the values lived in the community and not by virtue of a *collective contract* established from an *a priori*. The prudent legislator who knows his art would apply himself to discovering the moral principles underlying the people's mores so as to make them explicit under the form of commands. If the form of such legislation is the result of reason, its substance will come from the social fabric in appetite of a legal structure. The idea tinged with sociological positivism does not give reason all the extent of its role. As to the hierarchy of wills that traces human authority to the First Principle, it should not be arbitrary, but should rather rely on reason. It is to the latter that the obligatorily power to determine the law must belong, in accordance with the ontological order .

On the other hand, the obligation of the law is, to Aquinas, a moral issue which serves as a premise to demonstrate that the law is a product of reason. One can follow his reasoning as presented to in the De Veritate:

> Obligation says necessity. This word comes, indeed, from the Latin, *obligare*, and includes the verb to bind. That which is necessarily fixed to the place where it is and deprived of capacity to leave is properly bound. This implies a necessity imposed from outside, and not by nature. So, we do not say the fire is

bound because it necessarily rises into the air: that is a property which is essential to it.

However, we can conceive of a double necessity imposed by an external agent. The first one, which we called violence, is what compels absolutely on someone who suffers everything that the action of the agent determines for it. The second is a necessity of condition, that is to say, due to the assumption of an end. The *rights* of a person come from this necessity. It is something that is owed him or her, usually a freedom, because it is necessary for the performance of any duty imposed by law, whether it is specified positively or whether it belongs to one of the first principles originating from the natural law. Another example would be if someone imposes on another the need to act in a certain way, as a condition for obtaining a certain reward. The first of these necessities is inconsistent with the voluntary action which is free by nature; it can only be imposed on material beings. The second, on the contrary, imposes itself on the free will, as the necessity to choose a particular way, if one wants to obtain a certain good and avoid a certain evil.[107]

This text shows that forcing someone to act in spite of himself, takes away his external freedom to decide. (However, nothing can touch his inner freedom). The appetence of the end invites the free will to take the means that reason proposes to achieve it. There is, in that, a duty for the will, to which the appropriate right is due in order to accomplished it. To demonstrate that there really is a duty, the identity that unites the end to the ultimate good and to the ultimate perfection must be recognized. The source of this unity is found in the Supreme Being where the person finds its happiness, that is to say, the delight of its final perfection. Only the Author of human freedom could confer

---

[107] Thomas Aquinas, *De Veritate*, q.17 a.3 .

on it an obligation to the end which represents its proper good and its perfection.

It may be useful to consider, within this overall view of the law, the judicial theory of the interest law. Because a right is understood as a protected interest, there may not be any legal action if there is no special interest on the part of the applicant. However, there is no agreement on how to determine what constitutes an interest capable of being defended. Those who rely on Jean-Jacques Rousseau conceive of the nation as a social entity resulting from individual wills involved in a collective agreement. According to this ideology, the role of the State is limited to placing restrictions on the freedom of the contracting parties in order to prevent them from harming each other. Rudolf von Jhering represents this view. According to him, the law is designed to protect individuals and social interests by coordinating them so as to minimize the opportunities for conflict. If, however, the interests are confronted, he gives precedence to those of society. He writes, not without brutality that "this represents for us a series of spheres of delimited freedom, like menagerie cages surrounded by bars to prevent the wild beasts from devouring one another."[108]

A right, according to this idea, defends only the interest of its subject. In contrast to this view, there are those who give precedence to defending the interests of the collectivity. According to them, the judiciary cannot simply control the clashing of human activity through negative and prohibitive regulations. It is not enough to ensure the coexistence of competing wills, but it is especially necessary that they be ordered harmoniously and cooperatively for the social end, that is to say, the common good. The essence of the law is less to prohibit certain activities than to assist in directing and stimulating them. This

---

[108] Jhering, Rudolf von, *The Evolution of Law,* p. 355. (As quoted by J. Laversin in "Technical Information" *La Loi,* Descle & Cie, Paris, 1935, p.290.)

is the position of Thomas Aquinas, a position that is reflected in his definition of the law.

There are still those who believe, as does Leon Duguit[109], that there are collective rights only as the law sanctions. Since human wills are not incorporated into a hierarchical[110] order, the subjective right, which comes from the will of the leader, does not exist for thinkers who espouse this ideology. They recognize, however, that the tasks necessary for the conduct of society must be met by individuals who *exercise a right* due to the fact that the activity in question is legally protected. This lack of respect for nature and the destiny of the person, shows, in effect, an ideological sequel of the positivist sociology. According to the latter, from the point of view of society, the individual person has no existence. If it has one, it will be from the point of view of morality or of psychology and will be mostly recognized by the sociologist. Also, the legislature will have nothing to do with a person's conscience, since it belongs to an order that does not affect a right.

This idea taken to the extreme is obviously false, since many individual rights exist whose effects are not directly collective, but whose important consequences are necessarily attributable to the State. Mutual respect for individual liberties, for example, is a guarantee for the peace of the community. A synthesis between individual interest and that of social function had to be attempted and for this tentative we are indebted to Maurice Hauriou.[111] It was a question of reconciling the personal rights claimed by citizens and those granted on the basis of services rendered the State .

---

[109] Duguit, Leon, *Droit social et droit individuel,* A. Fontemoing, Paris, 1921, passim.

[110] A hierarchical order grants the leader the right to exercise his will on his subjects in accordance with the demands of reason and those of the end, that is to say, of the the common good.

[111] Hauriou, Maurice, Principes de droit public, *Recueil* Sirey, Paris, 1921, *passim.*

Being an artisan of major syntheses, Thomas Aquinas had already accomplished this task with the perfection of his art, as mentioned by M.-J. Laversin in the following text:

> In St. Thomas, synthesis takes place naturally, because he does not limit function in its general sense, to the strictly social function. For him, individual interests are based, ultimately, on the essential nature of things, on creative wisdom, and at this level, the duty of the individual is a function belonging to the universal harmony, situated in the order of Being (12 Metaph., lect. 12). That is why it was possible to say that the foundation of rights, is always duty itself. This word indeed overlaps the social function understood in the sense of immediate usefulness judged in relation to a human collectivity. The social life itself takes its value only because it is an indispensable means for man to realize his natural or divine[112] destiny. It is only part of the moral order, but an authentic part, which gives the State the value and the limits of its role.[113]

Recognizing the growing interdependence among men, Paul Cuche already foresaw, in 1919, the importance of legal interest:

> There is no doubt that interest is something that always comes in the synthesis of subjective right. But what is equally clear is that, due to the growing interdependence among men, the social function element is becoming increasingly important. The more society becomes integrated and organized, the more individual activities become intertwined, to the point where it becomes difficult for us to act by ourselves without simultaneously acting

---

[112] We will come back to this in the next chapter.

[113] Laversin, M.-J., « Renseignements techniques », *La Loi*, Desclée & Cie, Paris, 1935, p. 291.

104

for or against the others. The division of social labour being accentuated, we increasingly need others in the pursuit of our primary and secondary goals and, on the other hand, we become more apt to harm them by the changes in our activities, even within our legal sphere of activity... But the time comes when the legislator must be concerned about regulating the aptitude we have for doing harm to one another, as a result of interdependence, at least as much as for the need to cooperate. The day when the element of social function, included in a private right, reaches such proportions that public order would be jeopardized if this right ceased to be exercised in accordance with its function, the development of legal intervention and legal constraint must compensate for the unlikely increase of individual virtues.[114]

The principle from which obligations arise (understood as duties) and the obligations of rights (understood as dues), is the end. But the end itself must be due, for an act cannot be due to an end without the latter also. We see this clearly reflected in the following from Thomas Aquinas :

Having the value of a due, that is to say being obligatory, can be understood in two ways: either in itself, thus the end of a company is a due by itself; for example a doctor can procure the health of his patient, because it is a good in itself; or for something other than itself, for example, without which it is impossible to achieve an end. So, the doctor orders his patient's diet, because it is essential means for him to recover his health. On the other hand, that which is ordered to an end as a means of attaining it more easily or perfectly, but not as a necessary

---

[114] Cuche, Paul, *En lisant les juristes philosophes,* De Gigord, Paris, 1919, pp. 121-122.

means to achieve its simple realization, that has no longer the character of obligation... of a due.[115]

The specific ends impose duties and rights only as a intermediary means to attain the absolutely ultimate *end* where it must stop. That *end* reigns absolutely over our free activity, as it contains our integral good and our beatitude[116] when it is reached. Finally, this absolutely last *end* gives all others their reasons for existing. Therefore, in judging that an intermediate end rests necessarily on the ultimate end (which is a priority in the ontological order), reason recognizes that the first participates in the obligation of the last and that the power of the last is devolved upon the means of the first to achieve it. The proper role of law is explained in the same way as it is the means by which human action is ordered by subjecting the will of the agent to the direction of reason whose object is the Good identified as the ultimate *End*. Physically, the law summarizes the order of activities in order to submit them to nature. Morally, it is the rule offered to the free agent for the choice of his actions. To be effective, the law must be known to the agent in the form of "universal propositions, of those general judgments of practical reason, ordered to action."[117] Under its direction, human life can more easily direct itself towards the *end* which gives to all free activity its *raison d'être*, as the law guides us by indicating the conduct that we need to have so as to achieve the ultimate *end*.

As to nature, the connection between the law and the ultimate end may be narrow or loose, but it still represents an essential and necessary order. The consciousness of the suitability and the repugnance of free actions depends on the reason which judges

---

[115] Thomas Aquinas, *Quodlibetum*, 5, a. 19.

[116] According to Boethius, beatitude is "a perfect state thanks to the assemblage of all goods." (From *The Consolation of Philosophy*. 3).

[117] *Summa Theologica*, I-II, q. 90, s. 1.

them. The precepts of natural law, because they come from the judgment of practical reason are a value in themselves. Thomas Aquinas agrees to this when saying that "the moral precepts derive their efficacy from the dictates of natural reason, even if they have never been included in the law".[118] If this is about of a right or *de facto*, the relationship between the prescriptions and the dictates of the ultimate end refers to the positive law, whether human or divine in origin. The first principles of natural law are not explicit, because they are found only in the actions of a just man, as Aristotle stated. The legislator who adapts them acts by referring to the concrete life of his social environment and to the supreme authority of God who orders the duty of man toward his ultimate end.

It must be admitted that life in society is essential for the full development of the human life and for the common good that depends on it, at least in regard to natural groupings such as family, nation or city. That necessity for the common good requires the duty of every human being who participates in society to act in a way that assures the maintenance of its peace and prosperity. This is why there cannot be a society without a civil authority whose role is to safeguard the general interest. This authority is exercised by laws - legal expressions of order - for which it has the right to demand the obedience of its subjects. Since the social order is founded on the social nature of man, the authority and legitimate power which ascertains it, are also of this nature.

Some authors, as was seen, have taught that the law takes its power from the ruler's authority only when it is enacted with justice and wisdom. On this topic, Laversin commented while basing his thought of the teaching of Thomas Aquinas :

---

[118] Ibid.. q.100, a.11.

The command emanating from the ruler creates an obligation in as much as the means imposed on social collaboration become, for the subjects, *actually essential* for the moral perfection to which they are bound primitively. The law, which is nothing but that commandment expressed in understandable terms and enacted, is essentially a rational proposition that orders execution of the means chosen for an immediate end (the common good) and in the background with the ultimate goal of humanity. Without this supreme relationship, there could be threats or violence, there would be no obligation of conscience anymore. Thus, to perceive a relationship of means based on an end, is an action of reason as well for the person who is subject to the law as for the one who establishes and imposes it."[119]

This is not without problems. Since the common good of a particular group can be achieved in various ways, a choice between means is required. It is then that the will intervenes in response to the light of reason. The value of the legislation results from this choice that the will has implemented.

A solution to this question is given by Thomas Aquinas when he explains the ordering of the prudential act. The legislator exercises his prudential virtue when he chooses, among the many possible legislative proposals, those that contribute to produce the public good. Prudence facilitates the preferential option of the will among the different views that reason alone (since it is properly its role to judge relationships) could connect to the aim pursued. It is a matter of choosing freely without violating nature by doing so. It is still reason that gives choice its judicious character, by judging what is the best convenience of the law in its adaptation to the moral, economic and political requirements of a particular political group.

---

[119] Laversin, M.-J., *op cit,*, p.299.

The laws are made by the legislator according to his own faculties aided by political prudence. After making the most appropriate and expedient choice, prudence leads to the final resolution, the *imperium*. Practical reason adjusts itself to specific situations in its search for appropriate means of achievement; those that are more apt to overcome the inevitable difficulties. So, says Thomas Aquinas :

> It is from the will, that reason has its power of moving, for it is due to the fact that one wills the end, that the reason issues its commands as regards things ordained to the end. But in order that the volition of what is commanded may have the nature of law, it needs to be in accord with some rule of reason. And in this sense, the saying that the will of the sovereign has the force of law is to be understood; otherwise the sovereign's will would savor of lawlessness rather than of law.[120]

When the will aims at an end that sustains its desire, the intellect serves as its a principle while exercising its own activity because there is no mixing of the faculties. Reason, in a way, serves as instrumental cause, but it retains its specificity in their joint operation and its effect, where the action of the will is the main cause. Although distinct, these two faculties are so well married that those who would like to see them divorced cannot succeed in connecting freedom with requirement of the law. Without the light of reason which leads to the good that is the end of man, the will becomes a blind power that cannot bear the constraint of the law. It is then necessary to use the theory of Rousseau and impose the supremacy of the general will on the individual will.

---

[120] *Summa Theologica* , I-II, q. 90, a.1. ad 3.

The Thomistic thesis does not meet this difficulty, since it considers the will as a decision making power that has for rule the judgment of reason. This rule is rooted in being, for the first principles of practical reason derive from it. These first principles are requirements for *participation* in the First Being and their path traces all things of nature to the First Principle going through man. The law allows reason to discover these principles and obliges the will to act according to them.

Some law philosophers have based the legislative power on an omnipotent majority thus posing, by the fact, a sovereignty principle of itself. By contrast, on this issue, the Thomistic tradition holds the political system as optional. It does not matter whether that system be monarchical, aristocratic or democratic, provided that its legislation reflects the common good in accordance with the principles of practical reason. These principles that we discover in natural justice, are reflective of morality. The will to power could free itself from the dictates of right reason, but even if it would then claim sovereignty, it would lose its binding force. "What profit would there be for the political power to gain the whole world and forfeit itself in the process," one might say.

Safeguarding the principle on which the law is founded and which gives the legislator its legitimacy has led many a contemporary jurist[121] to substitute an existential law for the subjective law of a sovereign will. What is unfortunate from the point of view of this thesis is that we have often taken the social necessity as the sole support of this objective law. The result, in Canada among other countries, a pragmatic interpretation of this social necessity is left to the arbitrary judgment of the court or the legislature. How can we seek the common good without first considering the dignity of person and its

---

[121] Leon and Maurice Duguit Hauriou were previously named.

authentic[122] rights, beginning with the right to life? The natural law provides the first principles on which legal codes must rely to ensure the rights and duties from which is formed the social fabric of any well founded society.

There is still, among law philosophers, those who see society as an extension of the physical world, that is: "The interlink which forms a group from individuals follows physico-chemical model in which the composition of bodies is obtained by the synthesis of single bodies." Collective constraint implied by such an ideology is incompatible with a right conscience. It follows from such an idea that everything which is physically feasible should be allowed to be performed, although many possible things are morally undesirable.[123] In addition, this model shows a contradiction, because we cannot equate the free grouping of humans to the determined clustering of matter.

The natural law follows immediately from the universal order and the human law should be an explanation of this order. Wherever an order exists, a law can be abstracted from it. Thus, intelligibility, that is the unity and the very existence of the universe, subsists through the laws that govern it. Without the laws that establish the hierarchical order of its parts, the universal whole would simply be a heap. The intelligence that is reflected in this universe has its similarity in man who is said to be its microcosm. In as much as he is a corporeal being, man cannot escape the laws that make up the universe as a whole, but as long as he is spirit, he can rise above their determinations. As *artifex* he can abstract these predetermined laws to establish new unities, works of his own making.

---

[122] These are the means necessary for man to reach his ultimate end.

[123] These are the means necessary for man to reach his ultimate end. This will be delt with in *The human person and his rights*.

The normative law, which is the basis of the idea of natural law, derives its sense of submission (that the order of the universe obligates) by means of laws derived from that order. Since man fits into the universal whole as a part of it, the authenticity of his positive law depends on the philosophical conceptions that he elaborates regarding the universe and the order that appears in it. If "the law is a rule or measure of action according to which an agent performs the act or abstains from it[124]" it will be necessary that there be natures endowed with properties that are determinable in regards to their operations.

Can the legal reality be depicted otherwise than that of the Thomistic position just described? Those who adopt the positivist approach believe that it can be so. For them, the positive law results from necessities based on changing customs. It comes from evolving social forces which need to be represented as laws. Since, according to this view, the nature of man is either nonexistent or elusive, the law must rely solely on facts. Yet, left to the purely arbitrary judgment of a few judges or legislators, the interpretation of these facts of social life may not only be ideologically biased but, in addition, the operation itself necessarily tends to dictatorship. Such a power which is independent of the principles of right reason would have to fall under a sovereign will.

By contrast, to demonstrate their existence, we must identify the principles to which positive law must conform in order to be right and just. Some jurists have demonstrated that reality by referring to experience after finding that despite the changes that the law undergoes under the influence of place and time, one always find a common foundation, which can be compared to a sketch on which are appended the concordant features of diverse ethnic, cultural and

---

[124]*Summa Theologica* , I-II, q. 90, s. 1.

other groups. The characteristics that make this common foundation - the main one being the universal ability to establish rules of conduct - should, at least, allow for a descriptive definition that includes the notions related to the word *man*. The rules that are derived from humanity's power to manage itself socially and reasonably, are they not part of what defines man: his nature? Do we not draw from this human nature, some first principles on which are constantly founded the laws of all nations? There would therefore be a *natural law* on which would be founded *positive law*, which would be the result of legislation made by rulers in response to the necessity of ordering the groups for which they are responsible. The consistency of the Thomistic philosophy does not admit that the nature of positive law be otherwise; that it could be otherwise than a reflection of the universal order. Therefore, defining this aspect of order would suffice to establish the relationship between the law and the social facts.

In the introduction to this book, a passing reference was made to the present status of the positive law, recognizing its tendency towards a sociological foundation which claims to be scientific. Since this position denies or ignores the essential nature of man, it cannot accept immutable justice. So, it is important to examine the assumptions of such a position because it involves the privation of a necessary philosophical reason.

When social issues are placed in the domain of the experimental sciences, they are confined to the observation of phenomena regardless of their causes. Facts alone are noted, classifying them in view of discovering the conditions that will help to formulate a hypothesis concerning their survival and their disappearance. The results of these investigations are always alterable, being conditioned by the movement of phenomena and the different perspectives applied to their interpretation. Scientific theories, because they have for object the singular reality taken in its sentient being, never reach a full understanding of things. By contrast, philosophy judges things from the point of view of reason, by appealing to their causes. "The philosopher does not directly observe his conclusions: he establishes them as required starting points of the facts uncovered by science."[125] It was from this perspective that, in order to restore the rule of law, Pius XII suggested ways that are still valid today., The following is an excerpt from his speech Christmas 1942.

"The sense of law today is often altered and uprooted by the profession and the practice of a positivism and utilitarianism which are subjected and bound to the service of determined groups, classes and movements, whose programs direct and determine the course of legislation and the practices of the courts. The cure for this situation becomes feasible when we awaken again the consciousness of *a rule of law resting on the supreme dominion of God* and safeguarded from all human inconsistencies; a consciousness of an order which stretches forth its arm, in protection or punishments, over the inalienable rights of man and protects them against the attacks of every human power. From the rule of law as willed by God flows man's inalienable right to security before the law, and by this very fact to a definite sphere of rights safeguarded from all arbitrary attacks. The relations of man to man, of the individual to society, to authority, to civil duty; the relations of society and of authority to the individual should be based on a firm legal footing and be guarded, when the need arises, by the authority of the courts. This presupposes:

a) A tribunal and a judge who take their directions from a clearly formulated and defined code;

---

[125] Laversin , MJ. op.cit. p. 305

b) A clear juridical norms which may not be upset by unwarranted appeals to a supposed popular sentiment, or by a merely utilitarian consideration.

c) The recognition of the principle that even the State and the functionaries and organizations dependent on it are obliged to alter and to withdraw measures which are harmful to the liberty, property, honour, progress or health of the individual."[126]

Empirical science is based on the determinism of which nature manifests the evidence in its laws. At all levels of corporeal existence, whether mineral, vegetative or animal, we find an activity whose cycles are specifically invariable. Even in its own domain, scientific experimentation refers itself to the generally uniform behavior of each species of corporeal beings. Without this intelligible or logical reality which inhabits matter and its motion, no scientific law could be made and no technical application would be possible.

There is an axiom that every scientist must assume in order to formulate any scientific fact, which is *Unumquodque agot secundum quod actu est.*[127] Because everything acts according to what it is, it is possible for the chemist to base his experiments on the properties of various elements and the geneticist to predict the outcome of genetic mixtures. Not only do things have their proper operations, but they are also directed to their proper ends. These particular ends are finally and fully realized in the order of the universe. It is so affirmed by Thomas Aquinas commenting on Aristotle's Metaphysics :

All things are ordered in some way, but not all in the same way... Nevertheless, this is not without some link between them: there are, between them all, some relationship, therefore, a certain

---

[126] Taken from the *Catholic Herald*, London, January 2, 1942.

[127] "Everything will act according to what it is." Thomas Aquinas, *Against the Gentiles,* chap. 97.

order. Plants for example, are made for animals and the latter for men. So it seems they are ordered between themselves because all are ordered to a single end.[128]

Claude Bernard, as well, wrote that "it must be recognized as an experimental axiom that in living beings as well as in gross body the conditions of existence of all phenomena are determined in an absolute way. This means, in other words, that the condition of a phenomenon must always and necessarily replicate itself, at the will of the experimenter. The denial of this proposition would be nothing else than the negation of science itself."[129]

Thus, we see that the *right by nature*[130], as well as the natural law that reflects it, have as objective foundation a unity willed by the Supreme Being in view of bringing back to himself all corporeal beings participating of Him as one. This unity is woven by creating relations ordered to an ultimate end, though through the diversity of the operations proper to each species of corporeal beings. The natural law is an orchestration of *corporealistic* operations, ordered to the development of the essential goodness of each created body and subsequently to their common goodness. The order in question is one of relationship: the natures in relation to their proper ends; the means proper to these ends in relation to their appropriate operations; the hierarchical ordination of activities and of relationships between the species in relationship with the universal harmony and unity.

---

[128] Thomas Aquinas, *12 Metaphysics*. Lect. 12 .

[129] (*Introduction à l'édude de la médecine experimentale, P. 109.*) Hans Driesch, a biology scientist, also opted for a vitalist determinism in his writings, as he demonstrated especially in *La philosophie de l'organisme* (Editor Marcel Rivière , Paris , 1921). These two scholars have had recourse to the Aristotelian idea of *entelechy,* which they applied to known bodies to explain the finality inherent to their operations.

[130] As opposed to the "jus gentium" (law of nations) that relates more to the customs.

According to the formula left to posterity by Montesquieu, "the laws in their broadest meaning, are the necessary relations arising from the nature of things".[131]

Thomistic theodicy demonstrates the need to link the "rule of law" to the "supremacy of God" because of the need for a first principle to underlie the order regulating the universe. Just as the constitution of a country is developed under its prime authority, so the primitive constitution of the laws of nature rests on the Absolute Being. Everything depends on Him: the very existence of the corporeal beings of the universe as well as their natures and the activities they determine. In support of this argument, I quote the comment M.-S. Gillet who writes:

> The dynamic order of action must reflect the static order of being, and the good and evil of our deeds correspond to the good and evil of our nature through the intermediary objects consistent or inconsistent with its laws. This is why we say that human reason is the nearest foundation of rights and duties of which God, the author of nature, is the ultimate foundation; that the natural law is reducible to the eternal law.[132]

As was explained earlier, the emergence and evolution of participated beings - or corporeal beings dependent of the Supreme Being – is realized in conformity with the ideas eternally present in the plan of Divine Wisdom. The latter assigns to each of the corporeal beings its rightful place and the role it should play in the course of its evolution in time and space. There is nothing discordant in the work of the Creator-Providence and everything fits in the relationships described

---

[131] Montesquieu , The Spirit of Laws, (Esprit des lois, I, 1, Garnier-Flammarion, Paris, p.126 .)

[132] Gillet, Martin-Stanislas, Les actes humains, Desclée & Cie, Paris , 1926 , p.432 . Trans. J.-N. Chabot

above. Thomas Aquinas says it better when discussing Divine Providence:

> The natural necessity inherent in those beings which are determined to a particular thing, is a kind of impression from God, directing them to their end; as the necessity whereby an arrow is moved so as to fly towards a certain point is an impression from the archer, and not from the arrow. But there is a difference, inasmuch as that which creatures receive from God is their nature, while that which natural things receive from man in addition to their nature is somewhat violent. Wherefore, as the violent necessity in the movement of the arrow shows the action of the archer, so the natural necessity of things shows the government of Divine Providence.[133]

Thus, according to the transcendental order which has just been described, the interactions operate hierarchically, the most perfect powers compensating for the deficiencies of the less perfect corporeal beings. Even the failures of creatures, when they are deprived of their own development, contribute to the achievement of the universal whole. It is not according to the nature of the calf to be led to slaughter even before being weaned from the cow, but it is according to a more universal order of nature that man should kill some animals to survive. It would therefore be wrong to limit the application of natural law to particular factors regardless of its relationship to the universal order. The explanation may be exemplified as follows:

> As in the family, order is imposed by the precepts of the father which are, for each of the members, the principle of execution for those things which pertain to the good of the household, so also in the universe, the nature of each being is the principle of

---

[133] *Summa Theologica*, I, q. 103, a.1, ad. 3.

execution of its rightful role in the realization of the Universal Order.[134]

Giving the will primacy over reason upsets the order of created existence and causes, on the ideological level, adverse consequences for the common good . On the universal level, to admit that the essential order of corporeal beings results from an arbitrary will, independently of reason, would be not recognizing the existence of the eternal law. In human terms, this would be pulling the rug from under any attempt at justice. The law based solely on the merits of a free will, without the foundation of morality derived from the universal order, has not, in itself, the value of justice. The good, in such a case, would be what is allowed, and the evil, what is prohibited. We see what such a conception of the law may have for result when we consider the totalitarian regimes of the past century. These regimes sought to impose ideological values that often did not correspond to the norms that the natural law has inscribed in the conscience of their people. If we manage by dint of coercion to enforce such laws on people, what then remains of their personality? We recognize that human precepts may be contrary to natural law without our nature being changed for all that or our conscience being affected, but although coercion may fail to go beyond the threshold of conscience, what it will ultimately achieve is the corruption that comes from this kind of injustice.

The only moral obligation, if there is one, towards a government imbued with the voluntaristic ideology, is submission to authority. When a nation that claims to be "founded on principles that recognize the supremacy of God"[135] attributes to itself the power to create law

---

[134] Thomas Aquinas , *12 Metaphysics* , *lect. 12.* (Here , "family" is understood according to the universally recognized sense, that is to say, the sense that ascribes it to the natural order.)

[135] E.g. Canada. A claim made in preamble on its constitution.

without reference to natural law, the resulting dislocation cannot but affect the entire legal system. On the other hand, the legal system which finds the basis of its authority in the supremacy of God and recognized the hierarchical unity of will and reason will not judge arbitrarily because it participates in the very wisdom which is the eternal law. The legal principles that participate of the transcendent reality will insure that all the degrees of the created order retain their integral relationship, from positive law to eternal law, through natural law. Obedience, to be consented by the will, must first be justified by reason, that is to say, the order of justice must be recognized prior to willing. As for the moral obligation, it is founded on the necessity to maintain order and justice in order to meet the requirements of the common good .

There is, however, one important distinction to remember, regarding the personal precept and the law. The obligations proper to the vocation of each person is in the order of existence, since they receive their merits from the moral necessity to effectively execute what is commanded. On the other hand, the law belongs, rather, to the order of essence, where divine wisdom and human reason meet - because it applies to the form of relationship that the parts of the social body should take.

CONCLUSION

Intelligence or "*seminal reason*", which works it way through the evolutionary creation, is accompanied by love: the Creator God is love and this cannot be subtracted from his work. We see it in the elements that attract one another and unite to form a substance, such as H_2O for water. These substances in turn marry with one another to form more complex material such as carbohydrates. When life appears this love becomes more elevated with the introduction of sexual reproduction especially at the animal level where sensitivity is introduced. At the final stage of humanity the love returns to its divine origin, but it will adhere to its Creator's invitation only as a necessary free act of the will. Although free, man is still conditioned by his material composition and predetermined by the good. Since this latter predetermination comes from God, He alone can move the will towards the good. The Creator marries his Creation when man freely adheres to God's initiative in love.

In this context, Sertillanges writes that "*we are in historical times, and on this scale of duration the idea of species is firm: We can build upon it an edifice of thought and organize an action for it. Now, if the human species signifies something, please admit also that a species is determined not only by its structure, but still more by its behavior. An insect and another insect differ by the legs, the elytra or the mandibles. But Henri Fabre thought better to know them by observing their lodgings, their food, their couplings, their moults, their metamorphoses. The human species is no exception. If there is a human species, it is also characterized by its structure, but also by a natural behavior, by specific manners, and which will affect it entirely. The difference between man and animal, in this respect, is that the animal has natural manners and has precisely only that. Deprived of reason, it cannot give itself morals, free manners, as human beings do.* [136]

There is no existence outside of God. The Infinite being engulfs all beings. Even the evil angels owe their existence to God. According to their essence, they were created free of predeterminations, but they lost the freedom ordained for Divine Life when they created falsified determinations of their own free will. They have chosen not participate in the Eternal Life for which they were created and are consequently lacking the natural fruit of their nature and estranged from their true end. Spiritual beings have free will, that is, each one is free to participate or not to participate in the life of their Creator. Evil angels have refused to do so, preferring to exist within their own realm outside of God - so do human beings who damn themselves. The Creator tested the free will of our first parents. They were tempted and failed. Then, their condition was worse than that of the beasts who obey the laws inscribed in their nature. Man can create his own laws, but these often transgress his nature.[137] However, the author of life offers redemption by means of a New Way through which every individual of the human species has the possibility of entering and participating in the Divine Life. He who refuses to follow this New Way chooses the fate of the evil angels.

Creation, issued from Eternal God, was made to evolve so as to offer a home for the God-man who would return it to its eternal origin.

Reflecting back on the process of Creation we come to the realization that the divine Creator truly imprinted himself in his work. Although there is but one humanity (Man), it has the forms of two sexes (male

---

[136] R.P. Sertillanges, *La Philosophie des Lois,*, O.P., Éditons Alsatia, Paris, 1946. Trans. J-N C.

[137] "It is demonstrably clear therefore, that man is inferior to the beasts, in this life by the depravity of his nature, and in the next by the severity of the punishment." Bernard of Claivaux, *On the Song of Songs*, vol. 1, sermon 19, no.7, p. 145.

& female), the union of which creates the potentiality for a third, hence resulting in the existence of three persons, that is, father, mother and child. Man is consequently a trinitarian reflection. *One Man (species) and many persons (individuals)* helps us understand the Divine Trinity. Also, taken absolutely, we have the One Man, that is, the New Adam called Christ who represents the whole of the species, and thus Redemption is reflected in Creation. Everything from God is in his own image. The evolutionary creation attains its ultimate perfection at the incarnation and resurrection when God restores all to his Infinity. In Man the animal soul will die, but the spiritual will survive and, at the resurrection, a new body will be restored to the spirit resulting in a spiritualized body. *"It is sown a natural body; it is raised a spiritual body. It is written, The first man, Adam, became a living being, the last Adam a life-giving spirit. But the spiritual was not first; rather the natural and then the spiritual."*[138] God transcends His Creation, but the latter is from Him and in Him - that is, through Christ. (Roman 8: 19-22).

- Man as creature = body, soul, spirit accessible to divinity by participation
- Man as God = body, soul, divinity by essence
- The Spirit of the Word of God is his divinity
- The spirit of Adam is his capacity to participate in the Word of God's divinity.

Here appears the reunion of the Alpha and the Omega of Creation; here the First Cause meets the Final Cause. They are One.

---

[138] 1Cor 15:44-46.

www.ingramcontent.com/pod-product-compliance
Lightning Source LLC
Chambersburg PA
CBHW051442280526
45785CB00003B/1390